Congratulations

You probably picked up this book because you h.
want to know more about it. Little did you know you nave just become part of a revolution. A revolution to change the world of sales and marketing forever.

This book was written for a very specific group of marketing and sales professionals who design, build and execute the Purchase Experience process at trade shows, consumer shows, corporate events, private events and retail stores. The goal of this book is to provide people such as; Show Organizers, Association Managers, Branding Directors, Marketing and Sales Directors, Exhibitors, Booth and Sales Staff with the methodology and tools they need to execute an effective, efficient offering to their Target Attendees and Consumers. Best of all these tools don't require you to have a PhD. in statistics. All you need is a Purchase Experience venue and any booth or display space will suffice.

If you've ever exhibited at a trade show, consumer show, private event or even displayed your products in a retail store you know that the Exhibitor community is often misguided and shrouded in secrecy. The "successful Exhibitors" have vast resources and can afford to go to conferences and training programs where they learn from each other. These Exhibitors also have the resources to try the newest ideas and services out in their booth spaces. Once they gain knowledge from these endeavors they pride themselves on keeping it to themselves until the day that they become consultants and regurgitate their learnings for a price. And the cycle repeats itself.

But there is hope! There is a revolution going on driven by a change in methodology. The recent recession has left the industry scrambling for better, more efficient ways to use its' resources. Exhibitors of all shapes and sizes ranging from NEW EXHIBITORs using tabletops or 10x10's, to seasoned veterans in 20x20's, 100 x 100's and up are crying out for a lifeline. Fortunately, Martin Smith the leading subject matter expert regarding Purchase Experience behavior has answered the call.

The rewards for reading this book and implementing Lean Six Sigma are dramatically reduced costs and/or increased revenues which will maximize your Return on Investment (ROI). But there is more, you will begin to take control of your exhibit space and your events. Instead of the Show Organizer telling you what the proposed value of the show is you will tell them what it really is and how to improve it. This will change the face of the show world. **Congratulations**! You have just become a part of a revolution! Welcome!!!

The New
Lean Six Sigma
ORANGE BELT
for
EXHIBITORS
(and other marketing and sales professionals)
Masters Manual

The Methodology and Tools to successfully MASTER presenting product or service offerings at Trade Shows, Consumer Shows, Private Shows, Corporate Events, Flea Markets and even Retail Stores as a; Show Manager, Event Organizer, Retail Store Marketer, Sales Professional and above all as an EXHIBITOR

by Martin P. Smith

The New Lean Six Sigma ORANGE BELT for EXHIBITORS
(and other marketing and sales professionals)
Masters Manual

Published by:

Atticus Publishing and Holding

3256 Estates Ct. S

St. Joseph MI 49085

www.apahonline.com

or

www.bbmgo.com

First published in 2011

ISBN13: 978-0-9849414-0-7

ISBN10: 0984941401

REVL 020912

2nd edition

PRINTED IN THE UNITED STATES OF AMERICA

ORANGE BELT for EXHIBITORS

A tool set and methodology designed specifically to help companies master the use of exhibit spaces at trade shows, consumer shows, private events and even in retail stores, to display products and services effectively and increase ROI

Dedication

Special thanks to Max, Cathrine and Grace for sacrificing your time to help, encourage and love me and for making me throw my phone out the window when we are together. A special thanks to my wife JoAnne, for dealing with my insanity, for "gathering me" when I needed it, for keeping the family together, raising our children and for sticking by me when I didn't deserve it. I am blessed to have you.

To those of you who "ran me through as I stood at the edge", I hope you've seen this trash can dream come true and can bring yourselves to join the revolution.

Thank you George Angelov for giving me a sanity check on the statistics elements. I greatly value your help and friendship.

Lean

Orange Belt

Presented by
EXHIBITOR
magazine
in partnership
with Marty Smith

A Three-Day Innovation Series Learning Event

Six Sigma
Certification for Exhibitors

EXHIBITOR has been the authority
in all aspects of trade show and
event marketing, since 1982.
Our mission is to provide exhibit
and event marketing professionals
with the tools and education to
produce high performance programs
with measurable results.

Table of contents

Chapter 1

What Exactly is a
Lean Six Sigma Orange Belt?

First an overview

Lean Six Sigma or LSS merges Six Sigma methodology, which was developed initially by Motorola, with Lean principles that emerged from Japanese corporations.

In 1986 with Chairman Bob Galvin at the helm, Motorola initiated and perfected many of the Six Sigma tools and techniques. They decided that the traditional zero defect focused quality levels of the time weren't realistic and didn't provide enough granularity especially for their business transactions. They wanted to measure the defects per million opportunities and change their approach to quality to standardize it across all functions of the company. So they developed this metric of failures per million opportunities as a new standard. They also realized that they needed to institute a cultural evolution with this methodology in order to solidify the changes. The combination gave birth to Six Sigma. Six Sigma helped Motorola realize powerful bottom-line results ($1.4 billion from 1987-1994 and $15 billion over the next 11 years) in their organization. Subsequently hundreds of companies around the world have adopted Six Sigma as a way of doing business. The benefits have been praised openly by many of America's leaders such as Larry Bossidy of Allied Signal (now Honeywell), and Jack Welch of General Electric Company who allegedly bet that they could each implement Six Sigma faster and with greater results throughout their respective organizations. GE saved $12 billion over five years and added $1 to its earnings per share. Honeywell (Allied Signal) recorded more than $800 million in savings." Over the years both companies have documented tens of billions in savings as a result of their Six Sigma efforts which they like many of the larger companies are publishing in their annual reports under the watchful eyes of share holders and major accounting firms. More importantly these companies have evolved Six Sigma to include Lean methodology.

The term Lean was first coined by John Krafcik in a Fall 1988 article, "Triumph of the Lean Production System". Lean is the set of "tools" that assist in the identification and elimination of waste and "noises" in processes and systems such as the waste involved in the execution of a booth space awareness campaign. For example, suppose that an Exhibitor conducted an awareness campaign by paying a spokesperson or group of spokespersons such as the "Orange County Cycle (OCC) guys", to sign autographs in the booth in hopes of drawing in its' Target Attendees (TA). The OCC guys are notorious for being rude and offensive but for a stretch of time they were very popular and did a lot of trade show appearances at approximately $500k per appearance. If in the process of executing this campaign the Exhibitor surveyed TA's which revealed that the rude behavior displayed towards the Target Attendees left them feeling very dissatisfied and questioning the Exhibitor based on the company's affiliation with such unsavory characters, the nonvalue added activity would be eliminated.

Lean methodology also addresses a large scope of continuous improvement mechanisms including; waste identification and elimination, booth organization, vendor relationships, visual processes, error proofing, process standardization, culture changes and physical arrangement of the booth space to name a few. All of this promotes and ensures a synergistic and efficient flow of products and information throughout an organization. By comparison Lean focuses on identification of waste in a system or process and Six Sigma focuses on the reduction of variation or defects in a system or process.

These two disciplines when combined form a strong platform for the identification and elimination of errors that are systemically driving inefficiencies in the allocation of valuable resources. By reducing the waste created by variation in these systems and processes companies are able to improve the Purchase Experience for their Target Attendees and Consumers resulting in lower costs and/or higher revenues which maximizes their return on investment (ROI).

Lean Six Sigma and its tools are used to establish a standard and resolve any negative variations. With LSS the proverbial bar is perpetually raised throughout the Exhibitor organization. Lean Six Sigma is for all processes in an organization from the factory floor to show floor and it is easy to understand the advantages of it.

One of the biggest benefits is that LSS breaks an organization's reliance on fire fighting and redirects it to fix what's broken. LSS gives Orange Belt level Exhibitors the tools to resist the temptation to put improvements on hold so they can fight fires. They understand that if they don't change their ways they will continue to fight the same fires over and over again. LSS can transition an Exhibitor from a fire fighting model to a continuous improvement environment.

This is achieved because LSS is more than just a tool set. The Lean Six Sigma methodology focuses on being able to link the tools together into a logical flow so that data is moved from one tool to another and there is a synergy of upward momentum throughout the project. It's that synergy that increases the probability of problem resolution and success. It isn't an issue of one tool or method being better than another. It is simply choosing the correct tool for the job because a hammer doesn't fix every problem. With that in mind not every problem is fixed with the same LSS toolset within the methodology. For this reason Lean Six Sigma has evolved over time.

And LSS isn't just a quality system like TQM or ISO either, it's a way of doing business. As Geoff Tennant describes in his book Six Sigma: SPC and TQM in Manufacturing and Services: "Six Sigma is many things, and it would perhaps be easier to list all the things that Six Sigma quality is not. Six Sigma can be seen as: a vision; a philosophy; a symbol; a metric; a goal; a methodology." LSS is all of this and more. It is a structure for project management and a methodology which creates a culture of learning within an organization. It fosters continuous improvement both in people and the systems which make a business function efficiently. It is a mechanism for recognition that creates local heroes within an organization. It is a measuring stick for comparative analysis. It is a vehicle that transforms a corporations daily quotidian activities into a laboratory of exciting successes driven by experimentation. In effect Lean Six Sigma is a breakthrough methodology that drives change.

In 1964 Dr. Joseph Juran wrote his book **Managerial Breakthrough** in which he defines the difference between control, which is an absence of change, and breakthrough, which is change. Lean Six Sigma is a "breakthrough strategy". An Exhibitor, whether it is a one person shop or a corporate juggernaut, who accepts this definition embarks on a change program with the ultimate goal of eliminating defects and waste through change which leads to success. So how does Lean Six Sigma accomplish this?

Structurally speaking Lean Six Sigma typically has levels of expertise or "belts" ranging from;

- White Belt - Often referred to as "Champion's" this is typically a person who has achieved a basic understanding of the tools and methods. Often these are managers and executives who manage LSS people in a support role which is vital to the success of any LSS project. They assist in the removal of political and material road blocks for LSS projects and drive a great deal of the cultural change.
- Yellow Belt - this belt is for people who have been given a basic understanding of the methodology and a deeper understanding of the tools because they support other LSS people who are running projects.
- Orange Belt for Exhibitors- this is a belt program developed by Martin Smith, specifically focused on marketing and sales professionals, especially Exhibitors. They are trained using transactional examples (relevant to Exhibiting, marketing and sales) and are certified in the tools and methodology using Exhibiting, marketing and sales projects (instead of being asked to do projects in other disciplines) as a base.
- Black Belt - people who have gone through a more in-depth training process and completed projects to gain certification in the Lean Six Sigma problem solving methodology.
- Master Black Belt- a group devoted to transferring knowledge to the black belt community.
- Sensei - is a person who is not only proficient in LSS but is capable

of instructing others and implementing a Lean Six Sigma program (Dojo).

Participants achieve belts based on; their continuous improvement in their understanding of the methodology, their proven proficiency in the use of the tool sets and their ability to maximize the quality of their company's product or service offering with regard to their Target Consumers and/or Target Attendees by delivering an excellent Purchase Experience. To start the change process Exhibitors must find a way to intentionally make the status quo uncomfortable for everyone in the company because change is intentional.

It's more than just what an Exhibitor says, it's also what they do and how they project themselves through the show and the exhibit space. Exhibitors must spend time up front defining what Lean Six Sigma will mean in their shows with specific definitions revealing that the current way of doing things is not good enough. Keep in mind that when bringing in a new order, the best you can hope for is lukewarm support from those who are not doing well and those who are thriving under the current system will be outright hostile. Most people will perceive any change as a threat. So it helps to outline how you will promote and support Lean Six Sigma with the entire management team down through the booth staff in order to gain the acceptance of the deployment as it moves forward.

Note: For a smaller or new Exhibitor this may not seem as important because the road blocks and political environment is not as layered. But it is still critical to follow the steps outlined for the sake of;
- avoiding the trap of becoming an Exhibitor who just copies what other Exhibitors do and following the status quo

- creating a culture that promotes continuous learning moving forward
- making a booth space a laboratory for learning instead of a cost center that drains an Exhibitors resources
- defining metrics that will help in the decision process for allocation of resources moving forward

As part of this outline process the Exhibiting company starts by appointing a "Champion" who understands and addresses the change issues. Lean Six Sigma is not just about the quality of the booth design or the marketing program or the particular final product, it is quality of the Purchase Experience from cradle to grave. A perfect product delivered two weeks late is not Lean Six Sigma. A beautiful booth where the staff doesn't interact with Attendees and then doesn't follow-up after the show isn't Lean Six Sigma and the Champion must understand the issues that lead to failure and remove the road blocks for the team members.

A successful Lean Six Sigma operation next obtains buy-in from the team members on the clearly defined goals and objectives of the organization. Without internal agreement the change will never be "owned" by the organization and will always be an outsider's idea of what's best for the company. Buy-in also helps the Exhibitor to take the necessary step toward implementing solutions to problems through a structured iterative experimental process instead of operating in a fire fighting, trial by error mode.

This iterative experimental process allows LSS Exhibitors to identify and remove elements that; inject variation, cause defects (errors) in marketing and sales processes and/or do not add Customer value. The LSS program succeeds at defect removal by using a set of quality management methods, including root cause tools, statistical analysis methods and experimentation techniques. These are structured in a defined sequence of project management steps (DIMAIC) specifically targeted at Exhibitors and Marketing/Sales Professionals.

DIMAIC

The (DIMAIC) Pronounced (Di-May-Ick), is an acronym for six connected structural phases;

- Define
- Implement
- Measure
- Analyze
- Improve
- Control

Each step in the cyclical DIMAIC process is required to ensure the highest level of learning, best possible results and maximized ROI. The DIMAIC methodology is a data-driven quality strategy for managing projects and improving processes, and it must be an integral part of the Exhibitors quality initiative. Each of these phases has a corresponding tool set. The nuts and bolts of each phase are presented in detail in the following chapters one at a time. However here is a brief overview of each, starting with the Define phase.

*During the **Define** phase, the project scope is developed. This includes a project charter with goals and objectives, question mapping, brainstorming, problem statements, critical to quality characteristics (CTQ) and communication plans. It is during this phase that the Exhibitor will define;

- who the Target Attendee or Customer is
- what their requirements are for products and services
- what their expectations are
- what the project boundaries are (scope)
- who the team members will be
- where the stop and start of the process is

It is also the phase where resultant metrics (Y's) are clarified and theories regarding the potential outcomes are created. In addition, financial targets are quantified and assessed for return on investment (ROI) impact and comparative analysis against the performance metrics for the core business.

*As the event or show approaches the **Implement** phase, tools help manage the show processes and systems to capture the measurements and execute the experiments utilizing the defined factors. Gantt charts, implementation plans and process maps help to identify the critical paths to success and weed out wasted steps and resources. Failure modes and effects analysis (FMEA) defines the potential factors which can lead to failure and a ranking system is used to guide in the reduction of risky elements.

*At the **Measure** phase, data is collected from many sources to determine types of inefficiencies and defects. The various metrics are assessed for repeatability, accuracy, precision and quality. A myriad of tools and equipment such as; process mapping, data collection plan, basic statistics, capability studies, measurement system analysis, video cameras, surveys, registration/lead data, POS data and RFID are used to gather the necessary data from the show, event and/or experiments. Metrics are established that are focused on the Target Attendees. It is a fact that "people measure what they value". By creating Target Attendee (TA) focused metrics Exhibitors increase the value they hold on Attendees and improve the Purchase Experience dramatically. Although somewhat comparative by nature these TA focused metrics can be different for each show because these metrics are related to the Attendee centric goals that the company should always be working to achieve.

*During the **Analyze** phase the data collected is scrubbed to determine root causes of defects, identify sources of variation, reveal gaps in the current performance and goals in order to identify opportunities for improvement. Per the problem statement statistical tools such as; regression analysis, ANOG (Analysis of Good) and ANOVA (Analysis of Variation) help to identify the relationships among the variables (x's) revealing their independence or dependence on each other. The various x's that are causing the resultants (y's and Y's), to behave in an unacceptable manner are modeled out. The financial impact of the problem and the potential solution(s) to the problem are assessed. Hypothesis testing is used to verify or disprove the theories and assumptions the team developed around the causal systems affecting the resultants. Fishbone diagrams, 8D and why trees identify root causes and potential solutions. Customer survey results determine shortfall and perception issues in order to prioritize the opportunities for improvement.

*During the **Improve** phase, recommendations are made, processes are fool-proofed (Poka Yoked) and the next steps and additional experimental models that will be used to take the learnings and improvements to a continuous level are developed. DOE (Design of Experiment) tools create an inference space that will hone in on the specific factors leading to reduced waste, increased sales and higher ROI. Improvements to the future state process are created by designing creative solutions to fix and prevent problems. A new implementation plan is made for use in the next event cycle using technology and discipline to create innovative solutions.

*At the **Control** phase we institutionalize the solution(s). During this phase, quality tools such as mistake proofing, Poka Yoke, quality systems, and control charts can help to monitor the systems over time and verify special and common cause issues, in control and out of control episodes. It will also help Exhibitors to identify if the variation is within and between subgroups meaning if things are changing within days of a show or between shows. Control Plans serve as a platform for sharing learnings with the "Exhibitor Community" as part of the revolution of change. This will prevent the Exhibitor from reverting back to its' old ways and from making ill-advised, knee jerk reactions. It will also increase the organizations ability to make faster, more accurate improvements without spending resources wastefully. Controlling the improvements will keep the process on the new course. The development, documentation and implementation of an ongoing monitoring plan makes the improvements long lasting through the modification of systems and structures motivated through training and incentives. This will lead to lasting change for the organization and its' Attendee Customers.

In Lean Six Sigma organizations there is generally a certain mystique because the Exhibitor typically has gurus (Orange and Black Belts) who are skilled at creating satisfying Purchase Experiences that drive Attendees through the conversion process efficiently. They are adept at solving complex problems and driving lasting, high impact change for their Customers. They are committed to changing things and to making honest, candid assessments of their exhibit space, their processes or business. They are a sharp contrast to the Exhibitors who arrive at a show as fire fighters and trial by error copycats with absolutely no methodology for improvement through experimentation driven by goals.

Without specific goals or planning it is very difficult for the staff to execute successfully. Most exhibit designers spend resources making the exhibit space look nice without considering how the design will affect the behavior of the staff and/or Attendees. In measuring these Exhibitors historically, attraction rates (meaning the percentage of people drawn off the aisle and into the booth space) are around 30% or about one sigma. In the world of LSS a sigma of 6 means that the yield is such that the Purchase Experience only fails three times for every million opportunities. So for every million Target Attendees who pass-by the booth only two or three of them will not be drawn into the booth. In the manufacturing world companies operate at between three to four sigma, which means their processes yield around 93% to 99%. As bad as their manufacturing processes are for most companies their transactional processes are in even worse shape at (30%) one sigma. This is particularly meaningful if this massive failure rate is put into context. Imagine if flight takeoffs and landings failed 70% of the time. No one would fly. How would people react if 2 out of every 3 times they deposited their paychecks into the bank they were accidentally misplaced or entered into the wrong account. What would a home seller do if their realtor informed them that they were only speaking to 30% of the people who entered the house while trying to sell it. Very few situations would be tolerated by anyone at a one sigma quality level and it isn't acceptable as an Exhibitor interaction rate either not because I say this but because the "voice of the customer" says it.

Our research shows that the number one complaint of Attendees at events is that they can not find a staff person to talk to. Meaning as they walk the show floor entering and exiting booths, engaging with booth displays and picking up samples they encounter product or service offerings which they would consider using and/or purchasing. Unfortunately when they try to find a staff person to interact with in order to explore the nuances of the offering in greater detail no one can be found. If they do find a person they are either interacting with other staff people (clustering), eating, talking on their cell phones or they are a temp staff person who knows nothing substantial about the offering. The data shows that less than a third of Attendees (27% all show average, 21% for Medical shows) who enter a booth space interacts with a staff person face-to-face. Consequently not being able to have an intelligent interaction is the number one complaint of Attendees at shows across the board.

The number two complaint is that even if they do interact with booth staff people they do not get a follow-up after the event. The data here shows that less than a third of the people who interact or swipe a lead or have any kind of conversion activity in a booth get a follow-up from the company over the next 6-12 months. Think about what that means. Exhibitors pay money and allocate resources to go to an event (research shows that as much as 22% of a company's annual marketing and sales budget goes to show participation), where there are qualified buyers. Unfortunately the Exhibitors only talk to a third of the Attendees who walk into their booths and they follow-up with less than a third of the Attendees they interact with. This is a ridiculous and unacceptable failure rate and the main reason that nearly 40% of first-time exhibitors do not return to a show the following year. Without a defined Purchase Experience process with Target Attendee centric metrics and a systematic experimentation plan, failure is certain.

But there is a better way. If an Attendee goes through the Purchase Experience of the booth space the first time without any defects or mistakes, then that Attendee is much more likely to be a life long, *Loyal Advocate* for the Exhibitor. There IS a difference to Attendees between a Purchase Experience that has to be fixed to be right versus a Purchase Experience that is made right the first time. LSS Exhibitors have;

- Knowledge about HOW to make the Purchase Experience right
- Knowledge about how to continuously improve an Exhibitors ability to make the Purchase Experience right
- Knowledge about the Purchase Experience and the processes that drive consumption in the form of $Y=f(x)$ is vital to the optimization of the Purchase Experience for the Target Attendee and will maximize the return on investment (ROI).

Lean Six Sigma Orange Belt for Exhibitors will help to obtain this knowledge and deliver a great Purchase Experience. It will break down the activities of marketing/sales and especially of exhibiting into segments or "projects". Each project has phases that are used to direct the work of the company, Exhibitor and even the Booth Staff. These projects can be broad like the launching of a 250 event trade show program or contained like the introduction of a new staff person into the booth. No matter what the project and how big or large the scope, Lean Six Sigma methodology can help manage it with the DIMAIC process and tools. So the revolution begins with the first piece of the DIMAIC which is the Define phase.

Key Learnings

As an introduction one seemingly simple tool to utilize in the DIMAIC process is the "Key Learnings" tool. I say simple because it is simply a document that captures bullet point statements identifying something relevant, important, significant or even just interesting. These points reveal educational, helpful, informative or applicable content to the show or project. This can be done individually and put on one sheet or it can be done as a team exercise. If done openly and honestly this document will repay a hundred fold and it will be one of the most unifying pieces of the project. It will prevent the team from repeating mistakes and it will capture accomplishments and breakthroughs. It is a living document and should be done at each phase of the project. If key learnings are documented diligently doors will open that no one dreamed would open. Start with an open sheet like the example below. It doesn't need to be anything fancy. It just needs to capture the key learnings.

Key Learnings:

_____

_____

_____

_____

(Key Learnings Example)

Define ⟩ Implement ⟩ Measure ⟩ Analyze ⟩ Improve ⟩ Control

Chapter 2

Define Phase

Define the Exhibit

The "Orange Belt" LSS training and certification program for Exhibitors and the exhibiting community is a collection of tools and techniques which seeks to improve the quality of marketing and sales activity for product/service offerings. These offerings are displayed or exhibited in show, events and retail stores successfully increasing ROI. The first phase of the DIMAIC process is the Define phase. During this project phase an Exhibitor will define;

- the roles and responsibilities
- the scope of the project
- the team and its' objective(s)
- the form of the business case
- the Purchase Experience process

It is essential to the Exhibitor that all activity in the DIMAIC process is focused on the Attendees as **Customers** and their **satisfaction**.

cus'to˘ m • e~ r, n [O Fr. coustumier; LL.customarius, custom.]
1. a person who buys, especially one who buys regularly.
2. a person with whom one has to deal.

sat • is • fac'tion, n [O Fr., from L. satisfaction
    (-onis), from satisfactus, pp. of satisfacere, to satisfy.]
1. to gratify fully the wants or desires of; to supply to the full extent.
2. to free from doubt, suspense, or uncertainty; to give full assurance to
3. to comply with (rules or standards).

In order to truly satisfy Customers Exhibitors need to get to know them, to understand them and comply with them. To deepen the level of understanding an Exhibitor needs to capture their current level of knowledge about Customers often referred to as "Tribal knowledge", which can be a starting point in making improvements. Even though this knowledge may be only a belief, a feeling or simply a hope that has been passed on from generation to generation without considering the current Customer needs it is a starting point and from there they can dig deeper. Getting to a deeper level of understanding requires a tool to capture the current tribal knowledge and open the door for additional learning. This is best handled with a question map or Q-map.

Question Mapping (Q-Map)

Simply put a question map is a document that captures all of the questions of a project along with the corresponding answers, by date. It also lists the relationship these questions have to one another and consequently shows how each question links and flows together which ultimately leads to the deeper or "root question".

Key roles of question maps:
- capture key learnings
- identify problems
- direct the work of the project team
- assist in problem resolution
- prevent Exhibitors from repeating mistakes or failures
- assess the thinking skills of the team members and organization
- communicate within and between teams
- communicate to management
- transition information to other projects or teams

The root question is built on the observation that a person or organizations first reactions are often based on tribal knowledge and consequently brings to mind misguided questions. But if we can discipline our thoughts to look past those initial questions and ask deeper ones that are linked together, the questions themselves will lead to better results. Which brings up one of the first major Orange Belt mantras, "*questions should always lead and answers should always follow*".

One of the guiding principles of root questioning is that deeper questions result in better answers and broaden our learning or inference space. So the root question is about asking deeper questions and although there is no right way or wrong way to start the question map process here are some simple guidelines for getting to root questions in the Define phase;

1. Begin with "What" or "How" (save the "When", "Who" and "Why" questions for later phases). At the Define phase it is important to focus on the what and how questions and hold off on the when, who and why questions until later phases because it keeps the team focused and prevents finger pointing. The objective at this stage is to understand and scope out the project goals, develop a team with roles and accountabilities and to map out the process which is readily accomplished with what and how questions. The other questions can mislead a project at this early stage and can even derail it. A why question at this early stage can lead to dependence on tribal knowledge and even victimized finger pointing. During one project review an executive asked "Why are we even doing trade shows?". This why question put a negative spin on the team focus as they quickly became defensive in trying to justify why they did shows. In the end they took his question to mean that he saw no value in trade shows

and they decided to withdraw from some of them including one of the major shows of the year. In circling back with the executive it was discovered that what he really wanted to know was; "What value are we getting and delivering to our Target Attendees from these shows?". This question redirected the team to look for the impact their booth was having on obtaining their marketing goals and they discovered they could not accomplish them without the events. How a question is phrased leads to the answer obtained. Ask the same question in different ways to see if the same answer develops. Why questions at this stage are dangerous so they should be saved for the Analyze phase of the DIMAIC. When and Who question fit better in the Implement phase. Each of which will be covered in more detail in following chapters.

2. Use plural team oriented nouns like "Us" and "We" in order to create open exploratory brainstorming and build team chemistry. Instead of question like "What are you going to do to increase sales?" use "What actions can we take to improve the Purchase Experience for our Target Attendees and drive higher sales?" to stop the finger pointing and creates team unity. With competitors working to beat one another every day, the LSS team members really can't afford to be working against each other, too.

3. Create detail using action words directed at resultant (y's and Y's) metrics and Critical to Quality (CTQ) characteristics. (These are the final measurements which are driven by qualities that are fundamental to Target Attendee enjoyment of the Purchase Experience.) At this stage it is most helpful to use words that promote active learning driven by a measurement. This will allow the question map to

direct the teams work and it will also make it easier to assign results driven tasks to team members. Be sure to pick Y's (resultants) which are Attendee focused and realistic. People measure what they value so if the metrics are financially focused it will reflect that what the organization cares most about is money. If the focus is on Attendees the LSS Exhibitor will become Target Attendee focused. If the wrong Y is picked, the wrong answer will follow and it will send the wrong signal to the employees and Attendees. If the perfect Y is not known, report more than one Y. That increases the probability of having the right Y. Also, it helps keep the team from optimizing one Y while sacrificing another critical resultant that is not being looked at during an experiment. For example a question such as; "How many badges can we swipe?" is not as productive as "How do we create a valued Purchase Experience that will drive 40% of the Attendees (since 40% of the Attendees at the show are Target Attendees) who pass-by our booth to engage favorably with our new TZ-75 Fetzer Valve display resulting in increased awareness about our safe, new, innovative Valve?

4. Use a standardized format for the team. There are no right or wrong ways to capture questions. LSS Exhibitors typically capture their question in a box with black text and connect the questions that relate to each other with an arrow or set of arrows that show the flow direction of the questions. They put answers to questions below the box in red text and to put the date of the answer. The most important thing is that the team uses the same format and makes the document a living document. This allows the document to be passed on should the team change from year to year and it ensures that the learnings are archived universally.

5. Start with high level questions and link them until you get to a root question. By asking questions from the top down you will unify the team. I have seen many projects where the team was dysfunctional because some team members were asking high level question while others were already deep into the minutia. Once they agreed to hold off the questions in one area and focus their work on another area they were able to move forward in a unified fashion.

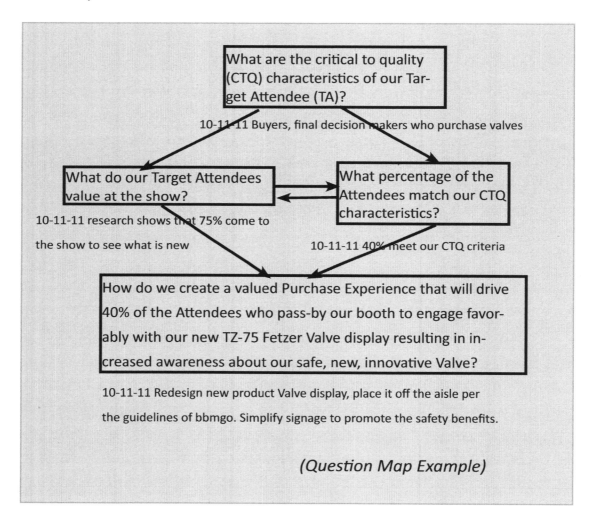

What are the critical to quality (CTQ) characteristics of our Target Attendee (TA)?

10-11-11 Buyers, final decision makers who purchase valves

What do our Target Attendees value at the show?

10-11-11 research shows that 75% come to the show to see what is new

What percentage of the Attendees match our CTQ characteristics?

10-11-11 40% meet our CTQ criteria

How do we create a valued Purchase Experience that will drive 40% of the Attendees who pass-by our booth to engage favorably with our new TZ-75 Fetzer Valve display resulting in increased awareness about our safe, new, innovative Valve?

10-11-11 Redesign new product Valve display, place it off the aisle per the guidelines of bbmgo. Simplify signage to promote the safety benefits.

(Question Map Example)

To better facilitate the development of an Exhibitor question map here is a collection of questions to consider which have been gathered from other Exhibitor Q-maps. These questions have proven helpful in driving the focus and bring unity to Exhibiting teams:

- What's the product?
- What feeling will our Attendees walk away with? Peace of mind? Order? Power? Love?
- What is an Attendee really buying when he/she buys from us?
- What part of this business opportunity is worth pursuing?
- What new products or prototypes are completed?
- What market area does this event open? Locally? Regionally? Nationally? Internationally?
- What business does the event hit? Retail? Wholesale? A combination of the two?
- What standards are we going to insist upon regarding reporting, cleanliness, clothing, management, hiring, firing, and so forth?
- How many potential buyers are there at the events in which we are exhibiting? Do we have this by event?
- What is the buyer population doing, growing or shrinking?
- What competition is at the show?
- How is our offering priced and how is it selling?
- What Is the future for our offering in this event, industry, region, marketplace?
- What is the anticipated growth of the event, industry, region, marketplace?
- What if any changes have occurred or are expected?
- What does our offering mean to Attendees, Target Attendees, the event, the industry, the region, the marketplace?
- What does our Exhibit mean to Attendees, Target Attendees, the

event, the industry, the region, the marketplace?

- How has our product or service offering changed Attendees lives?
- How has our product or service offering changed the show, event, region, marketplace?
- What kind of offering at all, would our Target Attendees like, and what would it look like?
- How would it feel to use it?
- What do TA's want a good offering to do for them? What benefits?
- What objections do our Target Attendees have to converting to loyal advocates for our offering, company, exhibit?
- What objections do our Target Attendees have to buying our offering?
- What would best serve our Target Attendees at the show?
- What could we easily give to our Target Attendee that he/she wants while also maximizing profits for the company?
- How could we give the Attendee the best possible Purchase Experience?
- How do we get the booth staff to take responsibility for that "best possible experience"?
- How do we get our staff people to do what we want?

Creating a question map can unify the whole team, focus their work and also get to deeper learnings faster. At the show the booth staff will be asked to create value for Target Attendee's and asking the right questions will help. But the staff will also need the overall goals, objectives and strategy for the Exhibitor and a plan of attack flushed out.

GOALS, OBJECTIVES AND STRATEGY

During every business cycle conditions vary, markets fluctuate and even people change. What works one day under given factors (x's) does not necessarily work the next. This means that businesses must plan for new challenges and changing conditions strategically. They need to develop a repertoire of responses and not only have their finger on the pulse, they must also be prepared when their heart unexpectedly skips a beat or even quits. This is best accomplished by documenting the goals and objectives of the Exhibitor in order to drive the strategy down to tactics which the booth staff can execute.

So, Exhibitors should start by focusing on a short list of goals and/or objectives. Without getting into a long debate about goals, objectives, strategy and tactics let me just say that Exhibitors should work under the premise that goals are short term in focus meaning at the show, and objectives are longer term in focus say over the next six to twelve months or over the course of a show season. With this in mind examples of goals could be:

- To clearly communicate the new innovative product/service offering to fifty Attendees per hour
- To deliver the new "Innovative Solutions" message to Attendees who pass-by the booth
- To display the five benefits to twenty customers per hour as a result of a recent merger
- To get twenty Attendees per hour to see the efficiencies achieved in shipping due to Lean Six Sigma implementation
- To show one hundred Attendees per hour the synergy achieved through the recent strategic alliance with an overseas partner
- To deliver a message to Target Attendees who pass-by the booth at

the show that the company is a big player in the marketplace
- To show off the new efficient manufacturing facility to four out of five Attendees (TA's) who pass by the booth
- To promote "made in the USA" to Target Attendees at the show

Longer term objectives might be things like:
- To announce that "We are the industry leader in Safety" at all 125 shows
- To instill confidence by showing consumers that the company has repaid the TARP money
- To change the public image from a "mom and pop" to a publicly held entity
- To create a global marketing platform
- To attract a larger base of distributors
- To look for collaborative partnerships with complimentary companies
- To create a networking stream in a vertical market

Whatever the reason(s) it is vital to the success of the Exhibitor that they set, clarify and simplify their goals and objectives. Make sure they are measurable and attainable. I have worked with Exhibitors who have stated generalized or unreachable goals like "create a global marketing presence"; this is not possible in an event that only draws local and/or regional Attendees, and no series of international shows will completely fulfill such a goal if the timing is too short and the plan is poorly executed. Also, how is it measurable? Typically the Exhibitors goals at a show are either ridiculously unrealistic or non-existent.

So start simple and write the goals down as clearly and concisely as possible. Don't be afraid to show them to other brain trust members and also be sure to get the buy-in of the booth staff prior to the event. This kind of idea sharing is necessary to achieve success so find a diverse, balanced contingent of right and left brain people to provide a sanity check. It is crucial to the execution that the staff is on board and clearly understands what the company is trying to accomplish prior to setting their own individual goals for the show. For now be clear, document goals and objectives and share them generously with the booth staff members.

Strategy types:
- Timing Strategy
- Preemptive Strategy
- Frontal Strategy
- Flanking Strategy
- Fractional Strategy

Migration Plan

A migration plan (sometimes referred to as an "as-is diagram"), is a map that takes the current condition of the Exhibitor (the "as-is state") and maps out a path to get the Exhibitor to its' ideal condition (the "to-be"). Depending upon the level which the map is working from individual paths can be established for different departments or events or areas of expertise. The actual map is a series of boxes with conditional statements in them which describe one state that is subsequently linked to an improved state box.

This tool helps companies to see where they are and where they want to be. It also makes the path visible which helps to identify road blocks or constraints that can prevent the Exhibitor from achieving their goals. It is great for project work because a migration plan clearly shows that there are no quick fixes for long term problems. Improvement takes time because change is not easy for any organization.

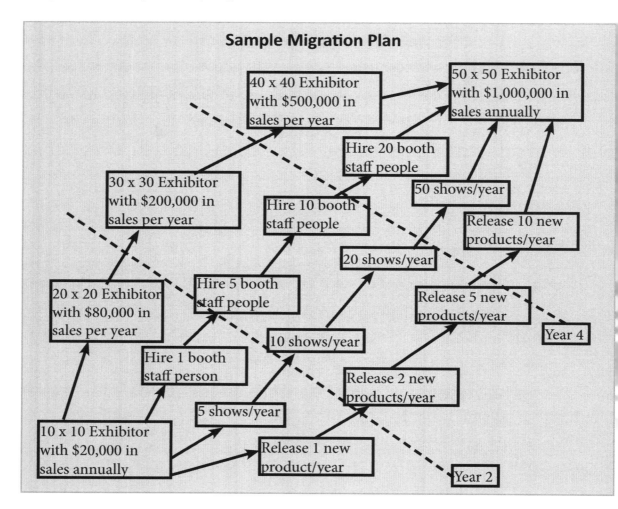

Migration plans like the one above allow Exhibitors to look into a dream space and strategically plan for the future. However this tool also allows the user to get into the granularity of each column and box in order to drive the goals and objectives down to tactical execution by the booth staff. In the end it is an excellent tool for planning, resource allocation and project management.

Once the strategy has been defined and the goals and objectives are documented it is time to start laying out the project. The tool set that helps construct the project into a defined contract is the "project charter".

Project Charter

The project charter is a document that captures some of the vital information about the project. It is typically a summary document that is used to clearly communicate to parties within and outside the team or even within and outside of the organization. The project charter like many of the LSS documentation should be viewed as a living document that changes and is updated as the project progresses through the different phases. Essential elements of a project charter include the project "statement of work". This is a summary document that is used to gain agreement on the depth and breadth of the project for all parties and areas throughout the organization. It is a summary of the project which should be signed off on by the champion of the project after getting buy-in throughout the organization. In effect it is the document that contractually binds the project and kicks it off. It typically includes a section that defines;

- what the project is about
- what the timeline is
- what challenges are revealed
- the Target Attendee goals and benefits
- the financial impact
- what the CTQ's are
- what the boundaries (scope) are
- what resources are needed
- what the deliverables are and the level of successful delivery
- who the team members are along with what roles they play.

After naming the project and recording the start date it is helpful to define the team members along with their roles and accountabilities. Referring back to the question map should give the Exhibitor some helpful ideas about what skill sets and levels of expertise are needed to assemble the right team members.

Good teammates can look right through one another and still enjoy the view. They appreciate each others gifts and strengths just as they are and they are personally accountable. They know that it is not about holding each other accountable, nor is it a group thing where people get together to discuss what did or did not happen. Good teammates know it is about holding themselves accountable for their own thinking and behaviors and the results they produce. They know how much better things are if they all try to mold and shape their own thoughts and actions rather than those of others and they act in accordance with their words.

Although different roles may be needed and some roles might overlap, here is a list of typical team member roles and accountabilities.

- **Champion**- Sets vision, clears obstacles and supports team. Is accountable for the ultimate success and sponsorship of the project by selecting the right leader and supporting and coaching the leader throughout the process. Accountable for project completion to Executive Decision-maker.

- **Project Leader**- Accountable for all project deliverables by leading the team to achieve its goals; has the authority and resources consistent with the project deliverables. Accountable for project deliverables to Sponsor.

- **Project Manager**-a member of the core team who is a key aide to the project leader and core team. Tracks budget, time and other administrative tasks

- **Team Members**- are the key to accomplishing specific project deliverables, assuming a variety of roles from broad support to special expertise: Dedicated "core" members or contributing members who devote less than 50% of their time to the project (but have at least 20% of their personal evaluation based on the project). All members assure that functional expertise and perspective are applied to a project and that contracted outputs are delivered on schedule and within budget.

- **Expert or Advisor Team(s)**- unbiased, expert viewpoint resource for team to leverage. May be found inside or outside company.

- **Functional Managers**- supplies expertise and resources to the project leader and project team as well as input into recommendations and implementation.

There are many different roles and this list is not meant to be all encompassing or a rule. The roles should fit the organization. If you are a "mom and pop 10x10 Exhibitor" you might be wearing every one of these hats. If you are playing every role document them so that as you grow you can identify which roles you need to fill first in order to move the business forward. You will also have a strong sense of what skill sets are required for the job and when it is time to fill the role(s). This information can then be plugged into the migration plan as the business develops.

Once the team is created and a strategy has been defined, it is time to define the project scope. Brainstorming is a key step toward successful LSS project completion. It gets everyone on board and excited about change and solving problems in the organization from within. When organizing a brainstorming session be sure to position the participants around the meeting room in such a way so that the managers are forced to sit intermingled with the booth staff and supporting employees to foster open communication. The question map can serve as a guide to help direct the brainstorming work of the team as they;

- describe the project
- bind the scope to prevent "project creep"
- define the project objectives
- establish the Critical to Quality (CTQ) characteristics
- predict success measures
- form success factors
- record key assumptions and tribal beliefs
- identify constraints
- determine deliverables
- assess the communication necessary for project success
- tabulate a budget
- schedule key dates - (taken from the GANTT)
- write down critical issues

The following pages provide a sample template for use as a scoping document. This is only a guideline and great care should be taken to adapt these tools and templates to the culture of the organization as well as to the nature of the project. This is not a one size fits all methodology and the tools are not meant to be used in a rigid fashion.

EVENT STATEMENT OF WORK

EVENT Name:

EVENT Start Date:

Team Members Chart

Name	Department	Contact Info	Role

Description of Project:

SCOPE:

OBJECTIVES:	CTQ's (see page 72)
1.	1.
2.	2.
3.	3.

SUCCESS MEASURES:	CRITICAL SUCCESS FACTORS:
1.	1.
2.	2.
3.	3.

KEY ASSUMPTIONS:	CONSTRAINTS:
1.	1.
2.	2.
3.	3.

UPCOMING DELIVERABLES:

EVENT STATEMENT OF WORK (Continued)
COMMUNICATION TRACKING

Audience	Topic	Method of exchange	Frequency of exchange	Date of exchange	Accountable team member

KEY DATE SCHEDULE

Milestone	Planned Completion Date	Revised Completion Date	Actual Date of Completion

BUDGET
- Actual To Date: $
- Projected Remaining Expenses: $
- Projected Total: $
- Budget: $
- Projected Variance: $

SIGNIFICANT ACCOMPLISHMENTS:

CRITICAL ISSUES:

Keep in mind that this is a living document and things will change. For example; The communication tracking portion of the sheet will help ensure that the right information flows within and between the Exhibitor team to maintain good engagement throughout the organization. The information that is flowing to a specific individual might change if the individuals' role changes. Consideration must be given to the listener in terms of what level of detail is appropriate to communicate especially as roles change so keep these documents updated.

In LSS methodology there are four key voices to learn to listen for. They are:

the voice of the CUSTOMER or (**Target Attendee**)	the voice of the **PROCESS**
the voice of the **BUSINESS**	the voice of the **EMPLOYEE**

Although it is true that an LSS Exhibitor should learn to "hear the voice of their Target Attendee Customer" in everything they do they must realize that some of the tools are better for hearing specific voices than others. One very useful tool for hearing the Customer is the VOC plan. This is a document constructed in order to define;

- Who the Target Attendee is (who uses the offering)
- What needs to be known about and from these Target Attendees
- How to obtain this information;
  - Surveys

- Focus groups
- Interviews
- Video Measurement and Analysis
- Attendee complaints
- Attendee objections
- Other Exhibitors
- Booth Staff interviews
- Show research

VOC Plan	
Who are our Target Attendees?	What do they value (CTQ) at the show?
What information do we need to know about them?	Where did we get the information on what they value?
What Target Attendees will we contact?	How will we contact them?

This will help to define the Attendee and the Target Attendee segments, identify sources of information regarding their wants, needs and likes, specify what Critical-to-Quality (CTQ) characteristics the exhibit and offering need to reveal to satisfy the needs of the TA's. Above is a sample of a VOC Plan which LSS Exhibitors find useful. Many of them use this as a section of their Q-maps.

Process Mapping

In order to hear the voice of the Process and start to look at the wastes and steps which cause variation in the system it is time to use the next tool to map out the steps and activities of the system. Since Lean Six Sigma is for the entire organization, and not solely for manufacturing or operations, every process needs to be addressed. Process mapping starts at the high or macro level of definition and migrates down to micro processes. It assigns ownership, creates responsibilities for the process owners who control them, and measures the performance of every process step.

A process by definition is a set of ordered action steps with inputs that lead to an output or resultant. Throughout the business, goals and objectives are achieved through process steps-- For example pricing while transactional in nature is ultimately driven by a series of process steps where inputs like current market supply/demand conditions, prices of similar product or service offerings, costs of raw materials/production, charges for logistic, fees for shipping...Etc., are evaluated. Ultimately these inputs lead to an output and a price sheet or model is delivered. How well the process operates is the focus of process management. Processes are managed to control what the Customer receives or comes in contact with before, during and after the show. (Note; in Lean Six Sigma the Customer may be internal as well as external).

Project management starts by laying out the steps using a Value Stream assessment table. (This is a table that defines what value streams are used with the different phases of the Purchase Experience process.) The value stream activities are matched to the specific phases of the Purchase Experience activities for the booth space.

Value Streams				
Pyramid Sales Phase	Extrinsic Value Streams	Intrinsic Value Streams	Relational (High)	Exhibitor Booth
PE Phase	Form	Function	TouchPoints	Activity
Awareness	Sight/Taste	Information	Samples	Presentation
Consideration	Sound	Application	Engagement	Demonstration
Preference	Touch	Education	Interaction	Objections
Conversion	Scent/Taste	Consultation	Affirmation	Invitation

For example; the first step is the Customer becoming aware of the business by stopping by the booth. This awareness might be accomplished by providing some information to the Target Attendee about who the Exhibitor is and what the benefits of the offering are. This might happen using a live presentation with samples. So Awareness building may be the first macro process management step for the Exhibitor. Key measurements might include the stop-by rate (meaning the percentage of Attendees who stop-by the booth compare to the number that pass-by the booth). This stop-by could include seeing the signage, watching a presentation or just hearing someone shout a message like " the annual census will begin in January please return your forms by June 31st"...Etc..

Awareness Start: The Target Attendees pass-by the booth.

Awareness End: Target Attendees stop-by the booth.

If the booth design is effective enough to draw a Target Attendee off the aisle and into the booth, the next step of the process might involve getting the Target Attendee to consider using the product. This is accomplished by providing applications of the offering that connect the Target Attendee to the product or service aspirationally and are best accomplished in hands on demonstrations. (Attendees are 39% more likely to purchase an offering if they hold it for at least 30 seconds) Key measurements might include the engagement rate (meaning the percentage of Attendees who engage with the booth properties). This could include picking up a brochure, seeing and participating in a hands-on demonstration of the offering...etc..

Consideration Start: Target Attendee engages with the booth property.

Consideration End: Target Attendee interacts with the booth staff.

Once a Target Attendee has stopped by the booth and engaged with the offering it is time to move them from consideration to preference. Getting them to prefer using the offering over their current provider requires deeper education about the details of the offering (costs, logistics, support...etc.) through relationship oriented sales. This phase requires face-to-face interaction with booth staff members who work to overcome the Target Attendees objections (88% of TA's who interact with a staff person face-to-face purchase a product). Key metrics might include the interception rate and/or the interaction rate.

Preference Start: Target Attendee interacts face-to-face with booth staff.

Preference Stop: Target Attendee is invited to become a loyal advocate for the company and the offering.

When a Target Attendee has gone through an interaction and all of their objections have been raised and answered it is time to invite them to the conversion phase. This involves moving the Target Attendee along the final phase of the Purchase Experience by providing affirmation in a consultation format. This macro process management step involves getting buy-in from the Attendee (referred to as "contracting" in LSS terms) while in the booth to allow the Exhibitor to follow through and complete the sale. Our research shows that 95% of TA's who agree to something verbally or in writing while in the booth will keep to that agreement. This could be an actual purchase agreement to exchange assets or it could be some other conversion activity such as; doing a site survey, performing an engineering inspection, swiping a lead card, setting an appointment...etc., whatever the conversion step is that closes the loop in the booth the TA is invited to participate.

Conversion Start: Target Attendee is invited to convert.

Conversion Stop: Target Attendee is closed.

Of course this is only the beginning for the company and it hopes that the process repeats in a never ending cycle or else they will lose Customers and they will not stay in business. LSS Exhibitors use this standard high level map to express the iterative process using numbered boxes to identify the phases.

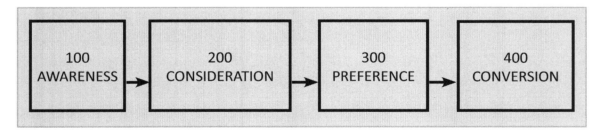

This is a high level map of the Purchase Experience phases that have just been defined. From here each phase is detailed out and numbered in keeping with the higher process phases. Some processes are more flows than steps but as a starting point it is helpful to get the activities and elements on paper in order to develop the skills of mapping out processes.

Continuing the example, the next step would be to put the detail from the exercise into boxes numbered in accordance with the phases that are going to be utilized at the show.

Here is an example of the awareness phase as a process with inputs from suppliers in ovals and steps in boxes. Note that the numbers are in the 100 series in keeping with the awareness phase.

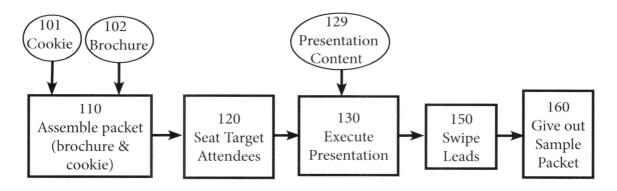

As you can see the process steps are captured as Target Attendees experience them -- and they are measured through the Customers perception of the process using metrics that are Attendee focused. This is how LSS Exhibitors measure their own performance because they bend the way they perform their processes to meet their TA needs. After all, it is the Attendee that is paying their bills and their salaries.

In the four macro process map phases above each of these phases may have two, twenty or even hundreds of micro or sub process steps. These micro process steps may operate in series or parallel or both. Other functions such as builders, set-up crew, carpenters, freight crew, booth demonstrators, presenters, technicians, sales and finance are intertwined with the process and sub process steps to achieve the end result.

Process maps should describe :
- process boundaries (scope of work)
- inputs (x's) and outputs (y's, Y's)
- Attendees, Target Attendees, Customers and suppliers
- major activities / tasks
- sub-processes (hierarchy)
- value added/non-value added/necessary to quality tags
- process owners
- Y's, y's, x's all leading to $Y=f(x)$ (resultants driven by factors)

Process maps are living knowledge documents which should grow and evolve over time as long as they capture what actually happens instead of what is supposed to happen or what you wish would happen. It helps to make a question map of the process. Document the decision process. Document what ideas are thrown out and why.

SIPOC

Another useful activity during the process mapping activity is to make a chart that lists some of the key elements (this is referred to as a SIPOC) which will be needed for definition of each process step. This starts by taking a specific process step and then listing the Suppliers or Service providers who are needed for the step in columns to the left of the process step. In the next column list the inputs delivered by the provider. To the right of the process step list the outputs from the step and the Customer who will benefit from this process step.

For example suppose during the Awareness phase samples will be given out to Target Attendees. The decision is made to package the sample (a Cookie) with a brochure and give it out following a live presentation.

SIPOC

SUPPLIER	INPUTS	PROCESS	OUTPUTS	CUSTOMER
Baker	Cookie	Give Free	Sample	Target Attendee
Printer	Paper Copy	Sample	Brochure	TA
Media Co.	Content	To TA's	Presentation	TA

The SIPOC elements can then be used to define the process steps. It is a standing record of what inputs, processes and outputs are relevant to specific Customer and Target Attendee types. It can help to identify activities or specific suppliers which might be combined or brought in house to reduce costs or drive efficiencies.

With the SIPOC in hand the steps of the process are put into a map using shapes and verbs. Using verbs helps people to see that there is effort and work required for each process steps.

In addition the factors (x's), measurements and resultants (y's and Y's) are noted on the chart and the process map is ready for evaluation.

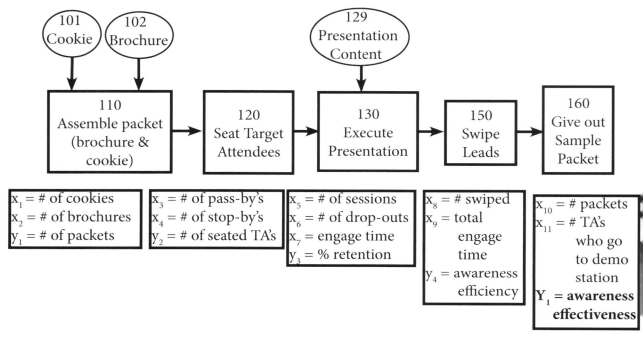

----------------------PROCESS MAP-------------------------------

(Note that this is a map at a deeper level of the 100 awareness phase so the numbers are all affiliated with that phase.)

There are standard symbols used for maps like this. Here are some of the more common ones and there are many more available on the internet or on our website *(bbmgo.com)*

- process steps are typically in rectangular boxes
- diamonds are used if they are decision points
- circles display inputs or end points.

In order to prevent the scope of a project from creeping it helps to list the steps at the level of detail the work is focused on. This will create boundaries and prevent the organization from over stretching the resources or from being disappointed with the results. Think of the process in terms of what work will be done and what will be measured. In the example above the following measurements will be obtained;

- the number of cookies procured (an "x" or input to the process)
- the number of brochures procured (an "x" or input to the process)
- the number of packets assembled (a "y" or output of the process)
- the number of Attendees who pass-by the booth
- the number of Attendees who stop-by and enter the booth
- the number of Attendees who sit in the presentation
- the number of presentations performed and the length
- the number who drop out of the presentation before it is done (which will help later in deciding if this is the right content for the Target Attendee (TA) audience)
- time spent in the presentation
- the number of packets given out
- the number of TA's who go from the presentation into a hands on engagement demonstration which will indicate if the presentation is effective in moving TA's from awareness into consideration
- the number of TA's who interact with the staff face-to-face which is an indication of the effectiveness in moving the TA from consideration to preference a ("y")
- the number of conversions (leads, sales, appointments...etc.) generated from these awareness activities which will indicate how effective the Exhibitor is in moving Target Attendees through the Purchase Experience. (However, each metric will coincide with the next phase of the Purchase Experience and each phase will need to be process mapped.) (a "Y" resultant of the process)

The process is now ready for a closing step in the define phase of the project. This entails getting buy-in from the team that the process has successfully been captured in its' "current state". The current state should reflect how the process really works. Not how anyone wishes it worked or how it was designed to work.

Process management means experimenting with the factors that drive a satisfactory Purchase Experience. It means measuring the steps and analyzing the effect on the Target Attendee. With process management the employee, the business and especially the Attendee wins. You may be up against decades of tribal knowledge and cultural brainwashing which will make the change difficult for some to accept. But when properly implemented through Lean Six Sigma methodology and tools (DIMAIC) the revolution will happen!

To summarize here are the steps to starting the process map activity during the define phase. In later phases you will analyze the metrics to create improvements, eliminate waste and non-value added steps and optimize the ROI of the system but for now take pride in the fact that you have mapped the current state.

Process Mapping Steps Summary

Step 1: Document the SIPOC
Write the;
- Suppliers
- Inputs
- Process
- Outputs
- Customer affected

Step 2: Document the steps and Set the Boundaries

- Write down the steps (post it notes will make it easier to move them as the process evolves during brainstorming) using a verb to explain the task description. The flowchart can be high level (in the hundreds) or very detailed (in the single digits), whatever is a sufficient information and detail level to understand the general process flow or detail of every action and decision point within the scope of your work
- Include all work (value and non-value added)
- Include the items that are driven by social-political capital
- Observe the process live or video the booth and watch it later
- Have other staff and even collaborative Exhibitors watch the process
- Don't change the process. Let the staff operate normally. Don't interrupt it if you want to know how it really runs. Observe and listen to what is going on.
- Define where the process focus begins
- Define where the process work ends
- Don't forget that when the correct work is chosen, the Champion will have no problem supporting it, as it will directly impact key initiatives.

Step 3: Put the Steps in order

- Place them in order of actual occurrence today not what it should be or what anyone wishes it was like.

Step 4: Use Symbols and Number

- Start with the basic standardized symbols:
- Ovals show input to start the process or output at the end of the process.

- Boxes or rectangles show task or activity performed in the process.
- Arrows show process direction flow.
- Diamonds show points in the process where yes/no questions are asked or a decision is required.
- Usually there is only one arrow out of an activity box and multiple arrows out of a decision diamond.
- Number the steps based on their order and in accordance with the larger process being considered. e.g....use 100's for processes and steps related to the 100 level awareness phase in the upper level process map.

Step 5: List the factors (x's) and the resultants (y's and Y's) for the steps and overall process being defined.
- x's are the things that will be measured at each step
- differentiate between things currently measured and things that could be measured (even if it can't be measured today, this will help with the "menu of metrics")
- identify things that can be measured accurately, repeatedly and precisely
- y's are resultant metrics from specific steps that will ultimately tell about bigger Y's. Y's are final output results in terms of the process being worked on. In the previous example the equation; $x_8 + x_9 = y_4$ would indicate the effectiveness of the presentation in giving away samples and delivering the Exhibitors' awareness message as part of the bigger "give free samples to TA process". Consequently the equation $y_4 + y_3 + (x_{11}/x_{10}) = Y_1$ would be an indicator of the effectiveness of the awareness phase activities in motivating Target Attendees to dig deeper into the Exhibitor product or service offering and perform consideration activities like engaging in a hands on demonstration.

Step 6: Get buy-in from the team

- Make sure there is consensus that the items (steps, measurements... etc.) are captured accurately.
- Make sure there aren't redundant or omitted items.
- Make sure the chart reflects it as-is not the way it should be or anyone wishes it was
- In the analysis phase the Exhibitor will determine if this process is being run the way it should be and if people are following the process as charted.

The purpose of process mapping during the define phase is to create a graphic representation of what is being done in order to help in the understanding of how it is being done. In later phases the process map will be used to identify what needs to be done to eliminate waste, reduce noises, perform more efficiently, allocate resources better and to pin point best practices to be implemented in order to drive improvements.

On the following page is a process map revealing the Attendee consumption process as depicted by an LSS Exhibitor. Note the addition of the diamonds which are used as decision point boxes. There is a vast array of symbols, icons and graphics which can be used to identify different elements of a process. Many of these can be found on the internet or on our website.

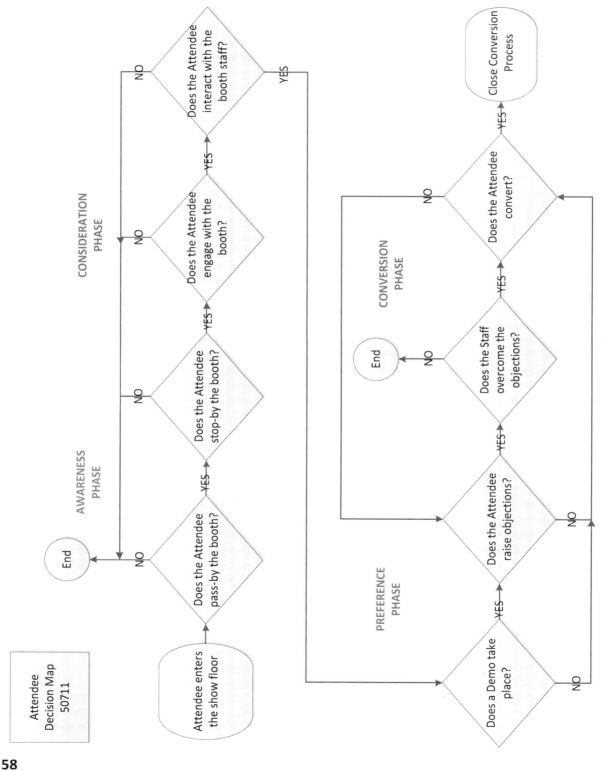

Attendee
Decision Map
50711

AWARENESS
PHASE

CONSIDERATION
PHASE

Attendee enters
the show floor

Does the Attendee
pass-by the booth? — NO → End

Does the Attendee
stop-by the booth? — NO

Does the Attendee
engage with the
booth? — NO

Does the Attendee
interact with the
booth staff? — NO

YES — YES — YES — YES

PREFERENCE
PHASE

CONVERSION
PHASE

Does a Demo take
place? — NO

Does the Attendee
raise objections? — NO

Does the Staff
overcome the
objections? — NO → End

Does the Attendee
convert? — NO

YES — YES — YES — YES → Close Conversion Process

58

What is needed to succeed at Lean Six Sigma

Lean Six Sigma Orange Belt for Exhibitors is a powerful methodology with effective tools built for solving Exhibitor problems and driving an exceptional Purchase Experience for Attendees. It creates breakthrough improvements, cost savings, defect reduction, greater Attendee satisfaction, and higher productivity and efficiency. To reap these benefits Exhibitors must .

1. Get Sponsorship and support from the highest level of Management
Champion team members must support the deployment at the top level of management. The must be involved in project selection, team and resource allocation, process reviews, self-assessment, brainstorming, conflicts resolution and event team rewards and recognition.

2. Lean Six Sigma Project Selection
Selecting projects that are tied to corporate initiative is vital to LSS success. The Exhibitor should perform a self assessment and determine their "as-is" state before laying out their "to-be" in a migration plan. The project scope should then align with this plan. It is also important that the project scope is managed and does not continuously creep further and further from its original objectives. Make sure that the projects are realistic given the resource allocation and make sure the project matches the key initiatives of the company. This makes it is easier to get support from the champion.

3. Project Team Selection
The right team members on the right project is a recipe for success. When looking at the project try to choose people from different skill sets

and areas of expertise in order to avert group think and encourage free thinking. Assess the thinking abilities of the team members to get a good mix of divergent and convergent thinkers involved. Don't just pick the people you like, pick the people who will get the job done and who you will enjoy learning from.

4. Make Lean Six Sigma part of the Culture

LSS isn't just a set of tools it is a way of doing business that is focused on Customers (internal and external). Instilling a sense of that in every aspect of the business from ideation to repeat sales and even in performance reviews will move the change through the organization faster. Take ownership of the LSS program. Make the training and mentoring more than academic exercises and statistical models. Transform people into subject matter experts, root-cause analysts, innovative problem solvers and process improvement gurus so that they can bring lasting value to the Exhibitor.

5. Reward Excellence

Business is tough and Exhibiting is exhausting. If Exhibitors don't take the time to celebrate their successes and reward their Orange Belts they will find that it is even tougher. Mark Twain said "I can live for six months on a good compliment", some people are highly motivated by recognition. So a little bit can go a long way. Besides life it too short and work will always be there so take a minute to enjoy the successes.

Building a Lean Six Sigma initiative modeled on these points will guarantee a sensational Purchase Experience will be developed for Target Attendees who will become lasting loyal advocates for the organization. This will drive them to purchase the Exhibitor's product and service offering. As the Attendee conversion rate grows the team will gain confidence in the marketplace and they will gain credibility throughout the organization. As shown in the Define phase of the DIMAIC there are a lot of tools and there is a lot to work on. Moving on to the next phase and introducing more tools and methodology will assist as the Exhibitor prepares for the opening of the show in the Implement phase.

Chapter 3

Implement Phase

The Show Opens

It is vital for Exhibitors to recognize that the Lean Six Sigma phases (DIMAIC) are a cycle in the same way that exhibiting is a cycle. Exhibitors arrive at the show painstakingly set up the booth space in preparation for the opening. Once the show opens many exhibit managers spend stressful hours fire fighting to deal with problems that arise in the booth. Items are misplaced or stolen, staff misbehaves, booth properties breakdown, displays don't work correctly, elements of the experience aren't cleaned or maintained properly. Outside of putting out fires the Exhibitor focus typically turns to the next show.

The association or show managers will conduct meetings with the Exhibitors to select space for the following year, sell banners and advertising, discuss sponsorship options...etc.. This is the cycle of the Exhibitor world which Orange Belt for Exhibitors emulates in the DIMAIC process. It is also why it naturally fits to follow the Define phase with the Implement phase. During the Implement phase the Exhibitor will establish;

- a plan for execution of the booth
- the measurements which will be captured during the show
- the logistics for setup and data capture
- the timeline for implementation of the event
- the roles and responsibilities of the Exhibitor staff and suppliers
- the specifications of the booth property and activities

Q-Map

To start the Implement phase it is always helpful to add to the question map (Q-map). In the Define phase the questions were What and How questions and direction was given to refrain from using other question types.

The Implement phase is logistics heavy and therefore requires the introduction of "When" and "Who" questions into the Q-map in order to:

1. create a timeline
2. prevent any procrastination
3. identify the critical path that must be followed
4. communicate to those involved in the show
5. clarify roles and accountabilities
6. help the team to see the time sensitivity of activities

Including these When and Who question types will prevent project and personal procrastination which is a failure mode and costly to all involved. This often occurs when Exhibitors spend too much time thinking about what they don't have or what they wish they had instead of making the most of what is in front of them and moving on. When they do the job with the tools they have they gain credibility and often receive more tools. Focusing on what isn't available is a waste of time and energy and it will immobilize a team. Instead capture the wish list items on the migration plan and leave them until they are attainable. Then turn the focus on succeeding within the constraints of the system and push the envelope by staying accountable. Exhibitors need to practice personal accountability in the small things throughout the project process to prevent issues from escalating. Using the Q-map can help.

I have witnessed many teams that were struggling until they reviewed their question map. Sometimes staff members are working on different issues and not in synch. If the team can put questions down and agree to table them while they work on other challenges together (with the promise of revisiting the other issues at a later date), they can often gain the momentum to move forward. Many of the questions that will appear on the question map that must be answered during the Implement phase are;

- What solution can we provide?
- How can we more creatively reach the customer?
- What can we do to find the information to make a better decision?
- How can we apply what we're hearing?
- How can we achieve success with the resources we already have?
- How will Attendees flow through the booth?
- What will they do in the booth space?
- What process will the Attendees go through in the Purchase Experience?
- What data will tell us how effective the process is?
- How will we obtain the data?
- What equipment is need to capture the data?
- Who will capture it?
- When will they capture the data?
- What booth property items does the process require?
- How much time does the process take?
- How many staff people does the process require to execute?
- How much space is required to execute the process?
- Where should the booth space be located to accommodate the process?
- How will our freight get to the booth? Who will move it?
- When does the freight need to ship? Who will ship it?
- Who will build and set up the booth?
- What facilities/services do we need? Electrical? Internet? Plumbing? Cleaning?
- Who will provide these facilities and services?

- When will setup start/end?
- What are the show days and hours?
- Who will do the tear down?
- What staff will work the show? When will they arrive?
- Where will the staff stay?
- What training is needed?
- Who will do the training? When?
- What will the costs be?

Sidebar on Budgeting

One way to work on the costs which will be necessary for ROI calculations is to establish a budget. Here is an example of a budget which has been developed by my exhibiting Customers over the years. I hope it is as helpful for you as it has been for them.

Establish A Budget

SAMPLE BUDGET

Exhibit Expenses	Items Budget	Actual
Booth Rental	_____	_____
Design and Construction	_____	_____
Graphics	_____	_____
Furnishings	_____	_____
Products for Display	_____	_____
Display Purchase	_____	_____
Carpeting	_____	_____
Total Exhibit Expenses	_____	_____

Shipping and Storage

Freight   _____   _____

Drayage   _____   _____

Exhibit Storage   _____   _____

Total Shipping and Storage   _____   _____

Show Services

On-Site Labor (set-up)   _____   _____

On-Site Labor (breakdown)   _____   _____

Electrical   _____   _____

Furniture Rental   _____   _____

Telephone   _____   _____

Carpeting   _____   _____

Signage   _____   _____

Cleaning   _____   _____

Security   _____   _____

Insurance   _____   _____

Computer Rental   _____   _____

Video Equipment   _____   _____

Florist   _____   _____

Audiovisual Equipment   _____   _____

Total Show Services   _____   _____

Personnel

Wages/Salary   _____   _____

Outside Help   _____   _____

Training

Total Personnel   _____   _____

Advertising/Promotion

Pre-Show Advertising/Promotion	_____	_____
On-Site Advertising/Promotion	_____	_____
Post-Show Advertising/Promotion	_____	_____
Total Advertising/Promotion	_____	_____

Travel & Entertainment

Airfares	_____	_____
Housing	_____	_____
Staff Meals	_____	_____
Client Meals/Entertainment	_____	_____
Hospitality Suite	_____	_____
Miscellaneous	_____	_____
Total Travel Entertainment	_____	_____

TOTAL SHOW EXPENSES	_____	_____

Returning to the question map, team members should do personal accountability maps and ask themselves questions like:

- How can I serve the team better?
- What can I do today to be more effective?
- How can I add value for Attendees?
- What can I do to better understand each person on the team?
- How can I be a better team member?
- How can I communicate better?
- How can I help move the project forward and prepare for the show?
- What can I do to hear the voice of the other team members better?

- How can I hear the Voice of the Attendee better?
- How should I greet Attendees? What should I say?
- How will I make the Purchase Experience satisfying for TA's?
- How can I drive continuous improvement?
- If I only have 30 seconds what would I want to convey to TA's?

Other Documents Needed

LSS Exhibitors are often accused of being punctilious list makers and checklisters. Truth be told they survive by taking copious notes and documenting everything. Through our research we have discovered that by documenting items the human mind becomes freed up to think of other things. In order to improve thinking and planning skills it is helpful to write things down and get them off your mind. LSS Exhibitors keep lists of everything and anything like; items that are needed when traveling, meeting room supplies list, key deliverables from suppliers, tasks that must be completed by each staff person, availability of critical items in the local show area, alternate hotels within a 100 mile radius of the show, key Target Attendees, training points...etc.

As part of the Implement phase there are several other documents that should be obtained and here is a list provided by other LSS Exhibitors;
- Floorplan - a map of the show floor showing where the booth is located as well as where collaborator and competitor booth spaces are located. It is also a good idea to identify key features of the show like stages, education areas, new product area...etc. and needed facilities like bathrooms, internet areas and eating areas.
- Booth layout - once the design has been solidified the layout showing the booth properties and design details should be documented

- Show schedule - defining the times and dates of show related activities.
- Staff schedule - making sure the booth is staffed and that staff members get sufficient breaks and time to explore the event is essential to success and can serve as a reward for hard work for the staff.
- Travel itinerary - travel itinerary for all staff members (hotel/flights... etc.) involved in the show should be documented. Many times I have seen team members lose, misplace or not know what their travel itinerary is only to arrive in a city not knowing where they are staying. Not having this information readily available and communicated can stress the team which can lead to defects.
- Equipment list - having a spreadsheet listing the properties, tools and materials needed for the show can be a stress reliever especially when things go missing or don't arrive.

MENU OF METRICS

With the question map in hand LSS Exhibitors can start to identify what data they will need and how they will capture it. Capturing measurement data accurately is the key to successful analysis which is vital to making improvements to Attendee satisfaction. Exhibitors measure what they value in order to understand it better. In the case of booth metrics they should be focused on Attendee. If you don't measure Attendees you don't understand Attendees and if you don't understand Attendees you are at the mercy of variation in their behavior.

During this phase the Exhibitor needs to set up the systems and define the metrics to capture at the show. One great tool for measurement decision making is the Menu of Metrics. This is a chart based on a brainstorming exercise where all of the metrics that the Exhibitor can, might and wishes they could collect are written down. These metrics are then categorized across the page based on what can be obtained currently on the left side migrating over to what the Exhibitor wishes they could measure on the right. Over time as metrics change and develop these measurements can come into play.

Side Bar

Fifteen years ago Exhibitors wished they knew how many Attendees walked past their booth, how many stopped by, how many engaged with displays and booth properties and how many interacted with their staff members. Unfortunately they didn't know how to do this. I started experimenting with video technology and developed a methodology using LSS to capture and analyze these metrics. I incorporated body language analysis to determine the signals Attendees were sending about their buying intentions. All of this resulted in a complete change in show measurement and analysis and the science around BuyingBehaviorMETRICS was born.

Over the past five to ten years radio frequency identification (RFID) and facial recognition softwares have opened the show world up to another level of measurement and analysis. Brainstorming and creating a menu of metrics with a wish list of measurements will spark the team to explore getting data that can really help the company to make better choices moving forward. Here is an example of a menu of metrics.

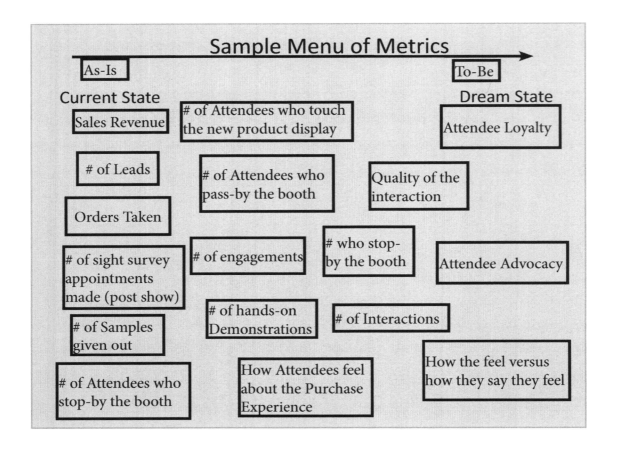

Critical Success Factors

During the Implement phase it is fundamental that the team understand what factors will determine successful execution of the show. This is essential because the measurements that are captured must correlate to a success factor or else there is no need to capture them. This will become more visible in the next tool which ties the items from the Menu of Metrics with success factors to produce the Data Capture Plan. In preparation there are typically six major factors that determine success for an Exhibitor they are;

Success Factors		
1.	Increase Revenue	Items that will drive revenue higher and increase ROI
2.	Decrease Costs	Items that will decrease the costs and increase ROI
3.	Enhance Attendee Experience	Items that add value to the Attendee Purchase Experience, drive repeat experience, create advocacy referral conversion
4.	Enhance Exhibitor Experience	Items that add value to the Attendee Purchase Experience, drive repeat experience, create advocacy referral conversion
5.	Understand Attendee Consumption	Gain an information regarding how Attendees consume the space in order to improve the Purchase Experience
6.	Continuity Components	Create data that can be used as continuity product for training and continuous improvement

This is not an end all list by any means and it should be customized by the Exhibitor but these factors have been painstakingly developed by other Exhibitors and have stood the test of time. Keep in mind that Attendee value is not created by success factors. It is created by satisfying CTQ's.

CTQ - Critical to Quality Characteristics

CTQ's are the characteristics that are vital to Customers. CTQ's at a show are often things like; seeing what's new in the industry. (Research shows that more than 75% of Attendees come to shows to see what is new. Providing displays that highlight the new products the Exhibitor is offering is a response to a CTQ characteristic.) CTQ's are also characteristics that the Attendee expects of the Exhibitor and their offering. If the Attendee expects the Purchase Experience to be satisfactory or the offering to be available for purchase the Exhibitor must provide these value streams as well.

Sampling Strategy

In LSS methodology, sampling is concerned with the selection of a subset of groups or individuals from within a population. It is used to assess and understand characteristics of the whole population and the groups within it. Sometimes defining a population is easy because the population characteristics are obvious. For example, the American Dental Association event has Attendee who are professionals in the dental profession. Sampling the dentists and/or hygienists would be an example of taking a subset of the whole populations. Sampling just female Dentists would be an even smaller segment sampling.

Sometimes Exhibitors need to sample over time, space, or some combination of these dimensions. For instance, an investigation of booth staffing could examine queue line length to a presentation area at various times. For the time dimension, the focus may be on periods or discrete occasions.

Typically Exhibitors are attempting to sample a group for the sake of effecting other groups. For example, an Exhibitor might study the success rate of a new 'super drug' display program on a test group at a small regional nursing show, in order to predict the effects of the display program if it were rolled out over a series of nationwide medical shows. Here the superpopulation is "everybody in the medical profession, made aware of this display" - a group which does not yet exist, since the display program isn't yet available to all.

Note also that the population which is sampled may not be the same as the population the Exhibitor wants to effect. Often there is large but not complete overlap between these two groups due to other issues and risks.

Sometimes they may be entirely separate - for instance, Exhibitors might study the staff's reaction to a presentation in order to get a better understanding of Attendee reaction, or they might study records from people from a different show or association in order to make predictions about other Target Attendees. (Recently I studied High School students registering for test in hopes of learning how Doctors would register. Getting the Doctors to do a test run was not possible but a donation to the school band allowed me to study the flow of 400 people in preparation for the real thing.)

Time spent developing an accurate and precise sampling plan is time well spent. It often raises issues and questions that would otherwise have been overlooked at this stage.

It's important when developing a sampling plan to understand the outer boundaries of the population. For example when exhibiting at a show with the hopes of selling boxing equipment for kick boxing enthusiasts, it would not be a good use of time to sample librarians at the American Dental Association's midwinter show because chances are good that the population is outside of the bounds of what the Exhibitor might hope to effect. So stay within the boundaries no matter what strategy is used.

Before determining which strategy will work best, the Exhibitor needs to determine the type of study being conducted using a population or process study.

- Population study - this type of study is designed to understand the characteristic of the people (Attendees) e.g. a population study would seek to determine the average number of Attendees at the entire show.

- Process study - With a process study, the Exhibitor is interested in predicting a process characteristic or change over time. For example, a process study would seek to know whether the Attendee behaves differently over the course of a show day based on changes to the Purchase Experience process. It is important to make the distinction for proper selection of a sampling strategy.

There are many different ways of sampling but LSS measurement typically uses: Simple Random Sampling, Systematic Sampling, Stratified Sampling and Random Subgrouping.

- Simple random sampling - In a simple random sample each Attendee has an equal probability of being sampled. This minimizes bias and simplifies analysis of results. In particular, the variance between individual results within the sample is a good indicator of variance in the overall population, which makes it relatively easy to estimate the accuracy of results. However the randomness of the selection may result in a sample that doesn't reflect the makeup of the greater population which will result in bias or errors. For instance, a simple random sample of ten Attendees from a the American Library Midwinter show will on average produce five government librarians and five public school librarians, but it is also possible to overrepresent government librarians (by getting 10) and under represent the public school librarians (getting none). This may also be cumbersome and tedious when sampling from an unusually large target population.

- Stratified random sampling is similar to simple random sampling but it is used when the population has different groups (strata) and the Exhibitor needs to have fairly represented groups in the sample.

Therefore, independent samples are drawn for each group in proportional to the relative size of the group. For example, an Exhibitor at a consumer show wants to estimate the average cycle time for a credit application process. She knows there are three levels of credit (high, low and cash only). Therefore, she wanted the sample to have the same proportion of high, low and cash only credit applications as the population. She first separated the population data into three groups and then pulls a random sample from each group.

- Systematic sampling typically applies to process sampling situations when data is collected in real time over the Purchase Experience process. Systematic sampling relies on arranging the Attendees according to some ordering scheme and then selecting elements at regular intervals through that ordered list according to some systematic rule - e.g., every fourth person to enter the presentation area every hour. A simple example would be to select every 10th name from a list of leads. As long as the starting point is randomized it and the Exhibitor avoids matching some underlying structure, it is easy to implement and efficient.

- Rational subgrouping is a sampling plan which will be used more effectively when you are doing experiments because it entails putting measurements into meaningful groups to understand the effect of the changes on these groups. It involves grouping measurements produced under similar conditions, which makes it ideal for situations where the Exhibitor is making changes as part of a designed experiment. For example if you want to see the effect of carpet color on Attendees, changing the carpet every hour and studying the Attendees in each carpet color group would be an excellent sampling strategy.

The goal of sampling strategies is to create subgroups in order to better understand the effects of variation on the Attendee Purchase Experience under changing conditions. When possible, subgroup Attendees under similar characteristics, time frames and conditions, for example; time of day, day of the week, day of the show, season of the show, trends in attendance, show location, booth location, product or service offering types, traffic volume, demographic mixes,...etc..

When determining sample size the Exhibitor should ask;

- Will the sample provide a good estimate of the true population mean? The more the better is the rule of thumb. If you don't study a large population you will make quick assessments and are susceptible to out group homogeneity effects and Type 1 or Type 2 errors. (The assumption that all Attendees are non-buyers or all are buyers based on a sample of interactions)

- How precise and accurate do you want to be? The greater the precision the larger the sample size.

- How well do you understand the variation and noises that exist and their effect on the Attendee Purchase Experience? The less you understand it the greater the sample size needed.

Data Collection Plan (DCP)

"If you hear a statement, your opinion is lowered by negative lies and raised by positive lies" -Dan Gilbert

One of the unfortunate truths about human beings is that we are gullible. Our opinions can be swayed and we can be mislead by lies. Right from the garden of Eden it was apparent that a little bit of truth mixed with a lie and we could be mislead. In addition to being swayed by lies we also quickly forget where lies, information, ideas and data come from. This "Cryptic Amnesia" or idea stealing is a memory function that prevents us from remembering the origin of cognitive items until we eventually believe they were our own. This memory misfiring allows people like Al Gore to believe he invented the internet or your boss to take credit for your ideas and work. It isn't always that these people are bad. Sometimes it is simply a fallout from the fact that after reviewing ideas long enough we start to believe they originated from us. And this extends to information and data at a show.

As Exhibitors if you don't remember where items came from you will begin to believe they are your own and even if the data is a lie, as long as it is a positive or reinforcing lie, you will be changed by it. You may try to discount the info if you know it is a lie but your opinion and your work focus will still be changed. Adding to this misdirection people (depending on the data source) do not typically verify the accuracy of the information they obtain which makes the situation even worse. So to prevent this memory function from misleading the Exhibitor LSS methodology utilizes the Data Collection Plan or DCP.

The DCP is a spreadsheet type documents that reveals what information will be captured before, during and after the show. The DCP combines the Menu of Metrics with the Critical Success Factors to define what will be measured, how much of the population will be sampled, who will obtain and collect the material and how that data will be gathered. The objective of the worksheet is to make sure Exhibitors measure the right or valued things and obtain creditable data that is reliable, repeatable and accurate in order to facilitate continuous improvement along the right path. Here is a sample template of the DCP and an explanation of the components.

	DCP Template										
Performance Area	Description	Data Source	Sample Size	Data Collector	Other Data to obtain	Data provider	When Data Obtained	Media Data Obtained On	CSF Tie

- Performance Area - this is the location of the booth that will be measured
- Definition - this is an operational description of the measurement to be taken
- Data source - this defines how the data will be collected
- Sample Size - the sampling plan will help to determine what volume of data will be gathered in relationship to the size of the total population and the amount of that volume is described in this item
- Data Collector - It is a good idea to allocate the task of collecting data to specific team members in order to drive accountability
- Other data to obtain - sometimes additional data that could or should be collected at the same time is available if someone asks for it
- Data provider - this defines what person or entity will provide the data. Sometimes this is a lead or registration company, a survey company or a measurement and analysis company like BuyingBehaviorMETRICS
- When data obtained - this defines the time and date of the data

gathering and delivery. This could be before, during or after the show

- How will data be collected - Sometimes data is on a disk or posted on a website or in the form of a physical report. Whatever the media it is documented here
- CSF Tie - No measurement is worth obtaining if it isn't tied to a critical to success factor. One of the reasons that data is not analyzed is that there is so much data that it overwhelms Exhibitors. Exhibitors measure what they value so by focusing on CSF metrics tied to Attendee value they diminish the amount of data to review which improves success

As you can see this document records the data capture logistics and keeps the information honest. Having integrity to the data will allow you to accurately measure things that are of value to Attendees before, during and after the show. It will also prepare you for the Measure and Analysis phases which requires accurate data as an input in order to deliver useful results and recommendations during the Improve phase. With this tool in hand Exhibitors can move on to a tool that assists with time management.

GANTT Charts

Exhibiting is a time sensitive endeavor. Activities leading up to the show are always time constrained and stressful. They are also dependent on one another which increases the stress level and accountability factor. This leads to the need for a tool set that allows; time management, connectivity of activities and tasks and accountability. The GANTT chart is the tool for this job.

A GANTT chart is a tool that is used to input specific tasks, assign a start and completion date along with a person or organization responsible for the completion of the task and also a link between the task and other tasks in the project plan. Once entered these items can be updated, viewed and even changed to reflect the progress of the project. More importantly a Gantt chart can be used to identify the "Critical path" of the project meaning the path that is so time sensitive that deviation from it will have a negative critical impact on the show implementation.

This allows the team to focus on the work that is vital to the show success and not miss deadlines. It also creates a sense of urgency for the completion of specific task items and accountability for the team members. A Gantt is a great tool for easy communication throughout the organization because it has a visual component that identifies what the status is of the project across a timeline.

There are many different softwares available for time/project management. There is no required LSS product but Microsoft Project is one of the easiest to use (any spreadsheet software like Excel also works although it doesn't give you any management tools). There are a multitude of free "how to modules" on the internet and a few on our website www.bbmgo.com so feel free to check them out. Overall some type of project management tool is necessary and vital to implement successfully.

In the following sample Gantt you can see how the information that is linked creates accountability and allows easy communication of the project status. These tools also allow for resource allocation and management which enables the Exhibitor to efficiently schedule the staff.

Sample Gantt

#	Task Name	Duration	Start	Finish
0	**Sample Gantt**	78.5 days	Tue 10/14/08	Thu 1/29/09
1	**1 Define**	14 days	Mon 1/5/09	Wed 1/21/09
2	1.1 Start Q-map	2 days	Mon 1/5/09	Tue 1/6/09
3	1.2 Initiate GANTT	1 day	Wed 1/7/09	Wed 1/7/09 2
4	1.3 Execute Event Q's Defined.doc with Customer	2 days	Mon 1/5/09	Tue 1/6/09
5	1.4 Finalize hotel/air logistics	1 wk	Wed 1/7/09	Tue 1/13/09 4
6	1.5 Collect Q's for DCP	2 days	Mon 1/5/09	Tue 1/6/09
7	1.6 Create DCP	2 days	Mon 1/5/09	Tue 1/6/09
8	1.7 Obtain Floorplan	1 wk	Thu 1/8/09	Wed 1/14/09 3
9	1.8 Create Tracking Sheet	1 wk	Mon 1/5/09	Fri 1/9/09
10	1.9 Create Camera Plan	2 days	Thu 1/15/09	Fri 1/16/09 8,9
11	1.10 Generate Communication Plan	1 day	Mon 1/5/09	Mon 1/5/09
12	1.11 Contact Convention Center Install Staff	6 days	Mon 1/5/09	Mon 1/12/09
13	1.12 Send Camera Plan to Convention Center Installation Crew	4 days	Sun 1/18/09	Wed 1/21/09 12,10
14	1.13 Final Team Pre-Event Review	1 day	Fri 1/16/09	Fri 1/16/09 2,3
15	1.14 Travel to Event	1.5 days	Sun 1/18/09	Mon 1/19/09
16	**2 Implement**	24 days	Tue 10/14/08	Fri 11/14/08

Legend:

Task	Inactive Task
Split	Inactive Task
Milestone	Inactive Milestone
Summary	Inactive Summary
Project Summary	Manual Task
External Tasks	Duration-only
External Milestone	Manual Summary Rollup
	Manual Summary
	Start-only
	Finish-only
	Critical
	Critical Split
	Progress
	Deadline

Project: Sample Gantt
Date: Mon 10/24/11

Lean Six Sigma is a comprehensive and flexible system for achieving, sustaining and maximizing business success. One of the tools designed to help prevent failure modes in the Purchase Experience process is the Failure Modes and Effects Analysis (FMEA).

Failure Modes & Effects Analysis (FMEA)

FMEA is a tool set that allows the Exhibitor to look at the design elements, compare them against the potential ways that the element could fail to deliver value and rate them. Items are rated on three criteria.

1. Severity - this is a measure of safety meaning, if this element fails how dangerous is the failure on a scale of 1 to 10. For example lets say an Exhibitor has an electric mechanical bull in the booth which they are going to let Attendees ride in an effort to draw them into the booth. During the ride one of the staff people could lose focus and accidentally crank the bull up too high. The resulting motion could throw someone off and injure them critically. This activity would receive a high severity rating.

2. Frequency - is a measure of how often this failure mode occurs. If something is likely to happen often it will get a higher number (again on a scale of 1 to 10) and a lower number if it is less likely to occur. How likely is it that someone will get thrown off the mechanical bull and get injured? One time for every hundred Attendee riders or one out of every three riders? The answer to questions like this determine the frequency.

3. Detectability - How does an Exhibitor know if the failure happens? If

no one can tell the failure has happened until it is too late the failure mode will receive a high score (again on a scale of 1 to 10). If it is obvious that this failure mode happens it is also very detectable and therefore receives a low number. For example if a warning light goes on well before the failure happens and it allows enough time for the failure to be averted it would have a lower number score. Back to the mechanical bull if the control knob is clearly marked so that it is obvious when the bull is set on high, the failure mode is detectable (low score).

For each failure mode a severity, frequency and detection number is allocated. These three numbers are then multiplied together to tabulate the **RPN** or **R**isk **P**riority **N**umber. Consequently items that have a high RPN are critical failure modes that happen often and are undetectable until it is too late. These would be items that demand some sort of corrective action or process steps to ensure that they are averted. These are also items that the work should be directed at first in order to keep the Attendees and staff from harm. Once actions are taken to diminish the failure mode the items are reassessed for severity, frequency and detectability and the cycle is repeated.

Here is a sample of an FMEA template and the criteria for ranking.

Outputs	Activities	Failure Modes	Effect(s) of Failure	Severity	Causes of Failure	Frequency	Controls	Detection	RPN

The FMEA is typically used in conjunction with a process map to identify and remove defects and failure modes. Here is an assessment using the previous example.

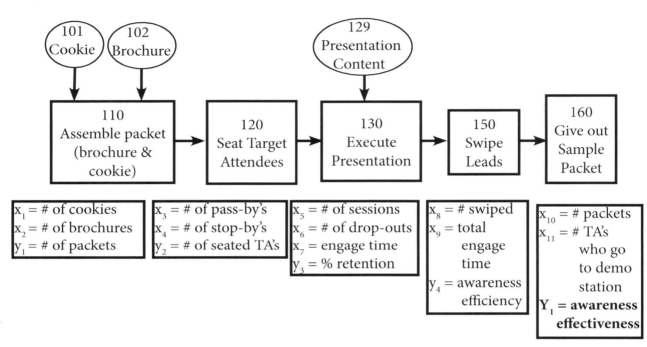

Process maps help to identify failure modes, the potential mechanisms that could lead to a defect in the outputs of activities.

Outputs - (y's or Y's) these are the deliverables from the process map. This process map should have the steps that encompass the show activities. Step 110 has an output of an assembled sample pack. Ask yourself "What is produced at this step?"

In our example failure modes relative to outputs are:
- the cookies do not arrive
- the cookies arrive but they are defective (damaged, broken, burned)
- the cookies arrive but not in sufficient quantity

- the cookies arrive but are not to specification (not individually wrapped, too large...etc.)
- the brochures do not arrive
- the brochures arrive but are not to specifications (smudged, torn, damaged)
- there are not enough brochures
- the staff does not assemble the packets

Activities - These are the functional activities from the process map that occur in order to deliver this output. Ask questions like "Who is doing what activities to produce the output?" Returning to the example there are three specific activities;

1. procuring the cookies
2. procuring the brochures
3. assembling the packets

Again ask questions such as "What is the opposite of the activities and/ or what is the lack of accurate completion or untimely completion of these activities?"

Effects of Failure - this describes what the potential impact of the failure mode is on the Attendee. Ask; "What is the impact of the failure mode and/ or what effect is produced when it is not accurately completed or not completed timely?" in order to determine the effects.

Severity Rating- as described above is a rating on a scale of 1 to 10 per these specifications;

1. No Effect - Failure mode has no effect on process/system and is not

detected by Attendees or Process Partners (staff/suppliers..etc.).

2. Very Slight Effect - Attendees/Process Partners not annoyed and effect detectable only by discriminating Attendees/Process Partners. Very slight effect on process/system performance.

3. Slight Effect - Attendees/Process Partners slightly annoyed and effects noticed by average Attendee/Process Partner. Slight effect on process/system performance. Manual work is optional.

4. Minor Effect - Attendees/Process Partners experience minor annoyance and effects noticed by most Attendees/Process Partners. Minor effect on process/system performance. Slight amounts of manual work may be necessary.

5. Moderate Effect - Attendees/Process Partners experience some dissatisfaction and effects are readily noticed by a majority of Attendees/Process Partners. Moderate effect on process/system performance. Extra manual work is required.

6. Significant Effect - Attendees/Process Partners experience discomfort and effects are noticed by virtually all exposed to Purchase Experience. Process/system performance is degraded. Partial loss of process/system functionality, but operable. Multiple resources tied up in extra manual work in order to keep process/system operational.

7. Major Effect - Attendees/Process Partners dissatisfied and it is difficult for process partners to avoid noticing the effects. Process/system is severely misfiring, but not in violation of legal guidelines and/or government regulations.

8. Serious Effect - Attendees/Process Partners very dissatisfied and notice of effects is unavoidable. Process/system is inoperable and compliance with legal guidelines and/or government regulations may be in jeopardy.

9. Extreme Effect- Process/system is inoperable, Attendee or Staff injury

may result and corporation is at risk for legal and/or government regulations violations and/or OSHA compliance issues.

10. Hazardous Effect - Process/system is completely, catastrophically, inoperable and unsafe to Attendees and/or Staff. Corporation is not in compliance with legal, OSHA and/or government regulations and/or compliance issues.

Causes of Failure - these are the mechanisms that could potentially cause the defect to occur. Continuing with the example process the cause of failure for the cookies not arriving could be miscommunication of the due date, Ask questions such as;

- Does this failure mode happen because of; Insufficient understanding of the importance of this activity and/or understanding of the downstream effects (especially in relationship to other tasks and/or priorities)?
- Does this failure mode happen because of; Insufficient understanding of the processes and/or the systems used to complete these activities?
- Does this failure mode happen because of; Insufficient information is available to complete these activities (correctly/accurately)?
- Does this failure mode happen because of; Insufficient time is given to correct/accurate completion of these activities?
- Does this failure mode happen because of; Insufficient understanding of how to use system tools to complete these activities correctly?
- Does this failure mode happen because of; System tools unusable or unavailable to complete these activities?
- Does this failure mode happen because of; Process partner input unavailable and/or inaccurate prior to completion of these activities? (Timeliness is also interactive here)

Frequency Rating - (Failure Rate is based on the % of the time the defect occurs on a scale of 1 to 10)

1. (Almost) Never - Happens Failure unlikely. No failures ever associated with almost identical processes.   [<1 in 1,000,000 or (0.0001%)]
2. Remote - Rare number of failures likely. Only isolated failures associated with almost identical processes. [1 in 100,000 or (0.001%)]
3. Very Slight - Very few failures likely. Isolated failures associated with similar processes.   [1 in 10,000 or (0.01%)]
4. Slight - Few failures likely.   [1 in 1000 or (0.1%)]
5. Low - Occasional failures likely. Generally associated with processes similar to previous processes which have experienced occasional failures but not in major proportions.   [1 in 500 or (0.2%)]
6. Medium - Medium number of failures likely.   [1 in 100 or (1%)]
7. Moderately High - Moderately high number of failures likely.   [1 in 20 or(5%)]
8. High - High number of failures likely. Generally associated with processes similar to previous processes that have often failed.   [1 in 8 or (13%)]
9. Very High - Very high number of repeated failures likely. 1 in 3 (33%)
10. Almost Certain to Happen - Failures almost inevitable. History of many defects.   [>1 in 2 or (50%)]

Controls - these are the current steps in place to avert the failure from occurring. Ask; "What things are done in order to keep this from happening?"

Detection Rating - evaluated on a scale of 1 to 10 if the process defect is apparent prior to failure.

1. Detection of Failure is Almost Certain - Current control(s) almost

certain to detect the failure mode. Reliable detection controls are known with similar processes

2. Very High - Very high likelihood current control(s) will detect failure mode before it happens
3. High - High likelihood current control(s) will detect failure
4. Moderately High - Moderately high likelihood current control(s) will detect failure mode before it happens
5. Medium - Moderate likelihood current control(s) will detect failure mode before it happens
6. Low - Low likelihood current control(s) will detect failure mode
7. Very low - Very low likelihood current control(s) will detect failure mode before it happens
8. Remote - Remote likelihood current control(s) will detect failure mode before it happens
9. Very Remote - Very Remote likelihood current control(s) will detect failure mode before it happens
10. Almost Impossible to Detect - No known control(s) available to detect failure mode

RPN - Risk Priority Number - multiply the (severity x frequency x detection). The higher the RPN the more risk is associated with this defect. The maximum possible RPN is 1000. A rating of 1000 would mean that the process fails every time and when it fails it is catastrophic but the failure isn't noticed until after it has occurred.

The rating system allows the Exhibitor to identify; ways the process fails to deliver a great Purchase Experience, effects of the defects on the Attendee, the likelihood of occurrence, the ability to detect failures. It will also allow Exhibitors to make decisions on what items to work on first. Typically anything that is a safety issue and endangers people (Attendees and Process Partners) should take top priority.

Decision Mapping

Another beneficial tool to use during the Implement phase is the decision map. This tool is used to identify the decision points in the process that the Target Attendees will be directed through during the Purchase Experience. By identifying these decision points the LSS Exhibitor can isolate the areas of work that the project will focus on.

When constructing a decision map dots are used to define points (nodes) where the TA will make a decision and solid lines are used to connect the decision points. For example as the TA (1) enters the show floor they decide to either go down an aisle (a) or not (b). This would be mapped as a dot and lines like this;

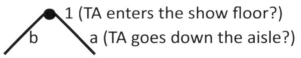

1 (TA enters the show floor?)
b a (TA goes down the aisle?)

At this point the TA has another decision point. They either pass-by the booth(c) or they don't(d). If they pass-by the booth they make yet another decision which is to enter and engage with the booth(e) or not to engage(f). At this point the LSS Exhibitor(2) decides to intercept the TA(g) or not to intercept the TA(h). Dashed lines are used to define (LOR) lines of restriction which define the process constraints and identify areas that are beyond the scope of the project. The decision map for these steps begins to take on a more complex shape as seen on the following page.

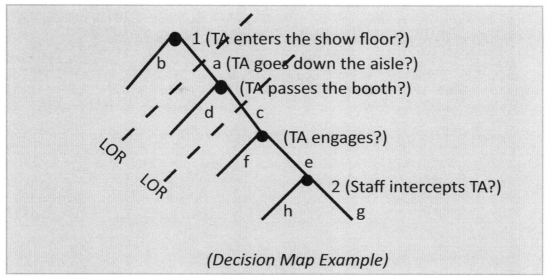

(Decision Map Example)

The LOR defines an area where the Exhibitor might want to work in order to drive an Attendee decision. For example there is a line of restriction if the Attendee does not enter the show floor. An Exhibitor might want to focus on changing this decision point by inviting the Attendee to the show with a prepaid registration badge. The LOR identifies constraints to the decision process that may or may not be changed by the Exhibitor. In later sections the decision map will be used to evaluate the effects of changes to the process based on experiments performed in the booth.

Checklists are very useful during the Implement phase. As part of the standard operating procedure (SOP) of setting up a booth from show to show it is extremely helpful to create lists which are checked off every time. These are useful in preventing people from forgetting things. This often happens when Exhibitors do show after show. It also helps to keep inventory at appropriate levels, it keeps the team accountable and the items can serve as metrics for the next phase. For example counting the number of sample packets can help ensure that there are enough for the next show but it also triggers the order of more prior to running out. In addition, it keeps a record of how many were given out which is useful for analyzing the effectiveness of the Purchase Experience. Here is an example of a checklist.

Checklist for Install

- Find the trunk (equipment)
- Remove needed equipment to begin checking process
- Check equipment functionality
- Power up (Power bars on table tops)
- Link to Server
- View Clarity
- Assemble Mounting equipment
- Move equipment to hanging locations (make sure all equipment is secure from theft)

Daily Checklist

- Check equipment functionality
- Power up (Power bars on table tops)
- Link to Server
- View Clarity
- Tours programmed, initialized, enabled, operational
- Check time/date capture on servers and camera storage

One LSS Exhibitor recently sent me this handy checklist which they use for their events.

Trade Show Action Plan

A. PRELIMINARY PLANNING

- Identify goals.
- List markets or market segments you wish to reach.
- List shows that cover your market(s).

- Obtain information-demographics, dates, locations, prices, special events, etc., from the managers of shows that interest you.
- Tabulate comparable data for each of the shows of your interest.
- Determine what results you would like to get from exhibiting at one or more of these shows.
- Define your general objectives for the show(s).
- List product(s) or service(s) you would display or promote at the show.
- Identify any special manufacturing or importing required.
- Determine if you have sufficient lead-time to get these items.
- Calculate how much booth space you would need.
- Estimate the number of people you will need to properly staff a booth this size.
- Calculate the cost.
- Prepare a draft budget for the show and compare it with the amount allocated in your over all budget for shows. Does it fit? If not, what compromises are necessary?
- Judge if you have enough information to confidently make a decision to proceed to the second stage of planning.

B. PRE-SHOW PLANNING

1. Make your plan
- Pick your show crew.
- Call a meeting to set firm objectives for the show.
- Determine how much booth space you'll need to meet these objectives.
- Confirm that your show crew is large enough to handle the project.
- Pick the show(s) that best serves your objectives.
- Set a theme for your exhibit and select items for display.
- Identify any special events you would like to host.

- Plan demonstrations, games, premiums, etc.
- Plan your advertising program.
- Choose a display company to design and build your booth.
- Plan your follow-up program.

2. Start the action

- Book your show space as soon as possible to get best location.
- Select booth design that meets your needs technically and financially.
- Order booth and set deadlines for final design, manufacture, and final approval.
- Start your advertising and promotion program. Wherever possible, integrate your promotion activities with those of show management and your trade magazines.
- With the aid of the exhibitor's guide from your chosen show manager, set up a chart showing deadlines for critical activities such as arranging transportation for crew and for your exhibit, ordering on-site services and
- tickets for special events.
- Arrange for show services including janitor, electrical, water, drayage, hotel rooms, parking, audiovisual, carpets, plants, furniture, lights, any other special requirements.
- Order items needed for display.
- Set up training program for booth staff.
- Design and order lead forms.
- Explain your lead follow-up program to your office staff and booth personnel.
- Coordinate your lead retrieval system with the show manager's registration system.
- Organize special events, demonstrations, press briefings, premiums.

- Do a dry run to set up the booth (if practical), and train your crew before it is shipped.
- Pack and ship your display or check that display company has done so.
- Ship lead form, literature, and general stationery items.
- Set up booth duty schedules.
- Make one final check that everything has been ordered.

C. At The SHOW

1. Before the show opens.
- Check booth set-up.
- Check that everything works and all supplies are on hand.
- Hold final training sessions on boothmanship and qualifying.
- Review schedules with booth staff and iron out any last-minute difficulties.
- Meet the press and place releases(kits) in pressroom.
- Check at-the-show promotions.
- Check demonstrations and special events.

2. During the show
- Hold daily reviews of progress toward objectives.
- Make any changes necessary.
- Take time to check out what your competition is doing.

3. When the show closes
- Secure valuable items.
- Pack all display items.
- Collect leads and dispatch to processing center.
- Dismantle booth, pack, and ship.
- De-brief crew as soon as possible
- Go out and have a relaxing evening.

D. POST-SHOW ACTIVITIES

1. Immediate post-show action

- Hold first evaluation meeting as soon as possible after the show before memories start to fade.
- Process your leads according to plan.
- Initiate active follow-up of leads.
- When your booth returns, check for damage and arrange storage.

2. In the weeks and months that follow

- Monitor follow-up program.
- Hold final review.
- Make recommendations for changes at future shows.
- Start plans for next show.

Many LSS Exhibitors use this "Exhibit Brief" and communicate it to every team member prior to the show. Notice the level of detail reported. This ensures that the whole team is informed.

Exhibit Brief	
Convention Name:	46th NORA Midyear Meeting & Exhibition
Convention Theme:	NOLA (network. opportunity. learn. advance)
Website:	http://www.NORA.org/midyear2011
Exhibit Dates:	December 5-7, 2011
Location:	Joseph Flannery Convention Center
City/State	LongBoat, FL
Booth Size:	20x80 Emmett Company

Number:	730 Emmett Company
Booth Type:	Island booth property to premier at NORA Midyear

Primary Products:	Variant Power Station Module
On-site Leadership (install and pre-con):	Zach Aroni., 212-555-2868 Genna Grenade, 222-555-7776
Booth Install Dates & Times:	Friday, Dec 2 – Sunday, Dec 4

Staff Pre-Con Meeting:	Sunday, Dec. 4, 5:00pm - 8:00

Westland Meeting Room (walking distance from Conv. Ctr.)
900 Camp Street, Long Boat, FL 70130
Light dinner served before or after attending pre-con

Exhibit Dates & Times:	
Monday, December 5	11:00 am - 3:00 pm
Tuesday, December 6	11:00 am - 3:00 pm
Wednesday, December 7	11:00 am - 2:00 pm

Booth Space Cost:	$89,555
Estimated Logistics Cost:	$12,500

Background: The NORA Midyear Meeting is the largest gathering of Game enthusiasts in the world. The NORA Midyear Meeting and Exhibition has provided professionals with a venue for updating their knowledge, networking with colleagues, enhancing their skills, and learning about the latest products and technologies.

Target Attendee Demographics:

2010 Meeting = 13,612 total professionals

8,913 Professionals including Director, Asst./Assoc Director,

Also: 4,375 Students, 188 Technicians, 3000 Game Enthusiasts.

New Product Introduction / Information: Andrew43 power station module

Marketing Goals & Objectives

Objectives: Highlight leadership position. Highlight innovation of power solutions, Display New ALYSSA model Processing Interface.

Corporate Key Messaging: Emmett Company is the world's leading provider of power technologies. Through its broad, integrated portfolio, EC is uniquely positioned to improving safety while reducing costs. The company is headquartered in Downers Grove Il., and has approximately 14,000 employees. Learn more at www.cousins.com.

Program Measurement:
- Sales: Number of badges scanned (only quality leads)
- Sales: Number of new, qualified sales leads generated
- Sales: Number of product demonstration stations
- Marketing / Communications: Booth staff / marketing evaluation
- Full traffic and timing analysis for Target Attendee Consumption

Industry Education:

For a full listing of Symposia, please refer to http://www.NORA.org

Tactics
- Convention Sponsorships: the Billboard/Literature Rack ($10k) and the NORA Midyear Meeting Microsite ($50k) as well as banner ads on NORA.org
- Advertising: Full page ads in daily News&Views; Hotel Door Drop; Corporate Window Wrap at the JP-ELLIE Hotel near the convention ctr $33k)
- Direct mail to all US pre-registered attencees http://www.TORI.pdf
- Meeting Room / Suite Scheduling: Alt Site has a product technology suite at the Hilton exhibitor suite on the exhibit floor
- VIP Tours: VIP tours before / after exhibit hours

Objectives;
1. Eight (8) commercial product demo station - (CATIE/KELLY) leads
2. M&Ms in individual sized bags on each counter - (LILI Corp. to provide)

Program Deadlines	
First Planning Meeting	09/27/11
Open Graphic Jobs & meet with Ad Manager:	10/6/11
Hotel & Badge Requests Due:	10/4/11 *$50 cancellation fee per room after 10/5/11
Med/Reg Approved Graphic Files Due:	11/3/11
Literature / Demo Product Orders Due:	11/10/11
Estimated Booth Ship Date:	11/25/11

Contact Information		
On-Site Booth Lead	Maxton Boy	555-1222
Demonstration Units	Gracie Girl	555-1212
Project Manager	Cathrine CJ	555-1234
Marketing	Mark A. Cronin	Cell 212-555-7776

These Lean Six Sigma tools will help prepare an LSS Exhibitor for implementation of the show. These tools are a starting point but keep in mind that exhibiting is an iterative activity and the DIMAIC process is cyclical. Once an Exhibitor goes through the first cycle they will find themselves coming back to this phase. On the second iteration they will be armed with an experiment designed during the Improve phase to take them to a deeper level of understanding about the Purchase Experience. This means that down the road they will incorporate an experimentation plan an FRD and other tools which will be discussed later during the Improve phase. But for now it's time to move on to the next phase which focuses on the measurement of the show.

Chapter 4

Measure Phase

In God We Trust, All Others Bring Data

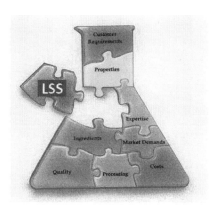

"When you can measure what you are speaking about and express it in numbers you know something about it, but when you cannot measure it, when you cannot express it in numbers, your knowledge is of a meager and unsatisfactory kind." --Lord Kelvin

Measuring the value of the Purchase Experience can be tricky. Goal driven activities during different phases of the Purchase Experience like getting Attendees; to see signage during Awareness building, to do hands on demos during Consideration, to interact during Preference or to transform into loyal advocates during Conversion can be harder to tie directly to sales especially if the actual purchase happens off the floor. To complicate matters, Exhibitors too often use inaccurate systems and processes to measure their effectiveness and direct their improvements. Many base their changes to the design and behavior in the booth space on subjective methods such as observations by team members. Staff will state that they think it "looks good" and based on the loose, unstructured observations of a few Attendees they will report that it is "working".

While these non-standardized observation methods are common they can also be extremely misleading especially if the method for observation is only subjective and not objectively systematic. When combined with other methods as part of a wholistic measurement and analysis program they can provide key insights and critical input to help gage the shows success. The Measure phase starts by looking at some different measurement methods.

METHODS:
1. Gemba Purchase Experience Tours (GPET)
2. RFID
3. Live Tracking of Attendees

4. Video/Audio surveillance
5. Survey - Pre Show, Entry/Exit, Post Show, Interview/focus group
6. Lead/Registration Data

1. GPET- One way to learn about the Attendee is to actively walk amongst them by registering for an event and experiencing the show as one of them. Participate in their activities. Be part of their culture. Go to the education and feature components as if you are a member of the Attendee population. Sample the products & services first hand and do some "mystery shopping" -(send in people to purchase the offerings).

Measure the experience by walking in the Attendee's shoes and getting immersed in the culture. It may seem easy, but it is deceptive. To do this effectively one must see the familiar as if it is unfamiliar because stripping away preconceived notions, tribal knowledge feelings and perceptions is not easy. Do this as a series of activities. Start small by passively observing the first time. On the second pass take a notebook and write down what is being seen and experienced. Avoid using judgemental descriptions. When making reference to something make sure it is qualified. e.g. the women wear expensive clothing (expensive compared to what?). In the next pass, try to add languages to the observations. Listen for key words or words that are unique to the subculture. Observe the Attendee body language and nonverbal communication but avoid sign language as it is really just a unique language. In pass number three, look for and document rituals or habits that are seen. Take notes but avoid interpreting the observations. e.g. (The Attendee was nervous.) is a label of the emotion and would be considered an interpretation. Instead focus on the observations e.g. (The Attendee swayed back and forth standing along the forcefield line off the aisle as the staff person talked.) that determined nervous behavior. Observe events and activities that are rituals. Kick off meetings, stage presentations, special events, master sessions...etc., that are unique to the subculture. Walk in and attempt to purchase the offering to see what happens at the point of sale and even after the sale.

2. Over the past 5 to 10 years, RFID (Radio Frequency Identification) has become more affordable. The cost of putting a chip on a badge and tracking someone throughout a venue has come down from hundreds of dollars per badge to under a dollar and the prices are still decreasing. Retailers like Walgreens have implemented systems to track promotional displays throughout its 5,000+ stores. The RFID tags are tracking when, where and for how long displays are being used in stores. Some shows have used them to try to track Attendees but with mixed results. The shows using RFID are obtaining so much data that they are in overload and have data paralysis due largely to a lack of a strong analysis methodology. Keep in mind when using this device that the amount of data and the diversity of the data must be driven by the questions being asked instead of by data output mechanism. If a solid methodology can be synergized with RFID, the reports generated could be very useful. RFID could open the door to a new level of measurement if it is tied to other data streams like the registration data. Knowing that a Target Attendee (as identified by the buying criteria from the registration process) has entered the booth is information that allows the booth to adapt to the specification of that TA. Displays can change, staff can intercept TA's and guide them through more relevant experiences. In short, the environment can transform to deliver the exact value streams needed to facilitate conversion. For Exhibitors, the value of RFID will continue to increase if it is used in correlation with other measurement technology. The combination of data streams is a game changer. One such technology that synchs well with RFID is video measurement.

3. Instead of registering as an Attendee one could select a sample of Attendees and track them as they move through the show or even through the Exhibitor booth. By doing this Exhibitors can examine where they go and what they do. They can look at what booths they go to and what activities they participate in. They can examine what properties they engage with and what staff they interact with. Timing studies can be done to determine how much time Attendees spend in these activities throughout areas of the booth, throughout areas of the show and even at the show itself (overall dwell time). Tracking individuals or groups can give great insight into how Attendees consume an event. This can be done with video or with live trackers. Unfortunately the data can be skewed if the live trackers are spotted. (Attendees may become upset if they discovered they are being followed.) Great care should be taken to ensure that this does not occur as it can also create a "Heisenberg or Observers effect" which happens when people know they are being watched. Once they know they are being watched they will behave differently.

4. Some shows and Exhibitors install video cameras in and around the exhibit spaces. The video is not only used to quantify traffic numbers and the amount of time Attendees spend consuming spaces, it is also being used to gain insight into behavior elements and staff effectiveness. Exhibitors learn valuable lessons from these observations which can confirm the effectiveness of booth properties as well as the activities executed at the show. The data can be used to identify challenges and visually provide examples that the staff team can use to make changes on the fly. This enables the Exhibitor to make enhancements while the show is still open instead of waiting until the next event.

The impact of video analysis is more than just the counting data. Categorizing behavior has helped to distinguish buyers from tire kickers. When an Attendee is ready to buy they will often perform very specific behaviors which are radically different from the behaviors of people who are just considering the offering. Behaviors such as "guarding behaviors" (activities like placing a hand on a product or blocking it off so that other Attendees can't get to it or even just holding onto it as if to say "this is mine") are meticulously identified and categorized. Video of these behaviors can then be used to train staff people so that they can be more efficient at helping Attendees through the Purchase Experience.

Video also allows Exhibitors to capture the event in order to do longitudinal research. Shows and Exhibitor spaces can be studied over any time frame in order to detect changes in Attendee preferences and/or behavior over time. This is especially helpful when doing experiments in the booth space (experiment models will be discussed in the Improve phase chapter). Large designed experiments or DOE's can be conducted where a multitude of factors can be manipulated in order to identify what factors actually drive Attendee conversion. Video capture is a great mechanism and perfectly legal in the United States (audio capture is very tightly restricted but video is not). Both are much more restricted overseas. So make sure you verify the legal constraints when going abroad. Video and audio increases in value when coupled with other data streams like surveys and registration data to answer specific questions.

Sidebar Camera Plan

Buying**B**ehavior**METRICS** specializes in measurement and analysis. Every form of data deemed appropriate per the LSS methodology is utilized. Some of these data streams are in collaboration with other suppliers who are more specialized in these techniques or the technology to execute them correctly. However since video is the main mechanism of the company here are a few tools and useful ideas for video measurement and analysis implementation.

Camera Plan

Simply put a camera plan is a tool used to capture where the camera(s) will be locate in the space and what the camera(s) will view. Sometimes this is accomplished through the use of a map with the camera views shown as arrows like the one below. There are a few things to consider when measuring with cameras.

Sample of a Camera Map

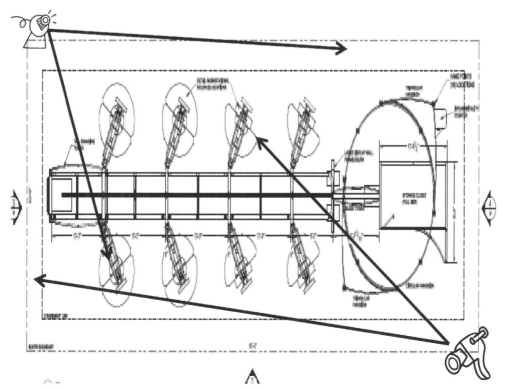

- Some cameras need power and a LAN (local area network) connection back to a storage device like a laptop or DVR. This can mean that the union people have to hang them which typically means there are OSHA requirements and safety standards to consider.
- If using hand held devices be sure to turn them on and off (recharge them) and change or download the media periodically.
- Make sure that views are unobstructed. I have often said, if you think its tough to work in a booth try watching someone work in a booth. I have spent countless hours watching video, counting, observing actions and looking for tell tale behaviors. The thing that makes it even more difficult is when the camera view is obstructed or off center. Good video shots lead to good analysis.
- Make certain that the camera is in focus. I remember an Exhibitor who filmed their booth but there was a flag that was waving in the booth. Every time the flag moved by the camera it would refocus the camera which rendered the video worthless (it served as a great example of what not to do).
- Always use cameras that have a time stamp synched to the video. It is so difficult to do any kind of analysis without a time sequence. Everything important in the booth happens at a specific time. Without the time stamp improvements are difficult at best. It is best if the time sequence isn't just a metadata file. It should be visible in replay.
- Most camera software allows the cameras to pan, tilt and zoom which makes it possible to change views throughout the show. This is very useful for capturing a multitude of metrics and behaviors but it also brings on some other issues. A document must be used to reflect the changes to the camera view by time and date. If the times

and dates of the changes are not captured an Exhibitor will spend endless hours searching through the video looking for the video angles that capture the metrics desired. With this in mind a camera change plan is also included in the camera plan. This table allows Exhibitors to keep track of the camera angles and where the files with the video are stored (location of footage).

Sample Camera Change Plan				
Date	Time	Camera #	View	Location of footage

It is also a good idea to include the SOP (Standard Operating Procedure) for the camera which outlines the operation of the camera system and even a checklist of things to verify daily like the one below.

Daily Checklist

- Check equipment functionality
- Power up (Power bars on table tops)
- Link to Server
- Full Motion P/T/Z
- View Clarity/Tours programmed, initialized, enabled, operational
- No tours for stationary cameras
- Enabled for correct day of show/Check time/date capture on servers and camera storage
- Files saving properly to disk/File sizes are correct
- Focusing correctly
- Execute panorama of show

---

5. Another mechanism that Exhibitors can rely on is surveys or questionnaires. Surveys, focus groups and other response oriented research is valuable for gaining insight into what Attendees remember, feel, see and think at a show. It can also be very useful for identifying pre show intentions and post show decisions. The three critical things to remember about these data streams is that:

- The questions can skew the results. As stated "questions lead and answers follow" holds true. To be good at survey work one has to realize that: the way a question is asked, the type of question being asked, the environment the question is being asked in...etc., can influence the answers. Many Exhibitors believe they can do survey work just by asking a few simple questions only to find out that they led the Attendee into the answer by the way they asked it, or they surveyed a sample of the population that skewed the data or a host of other mistakes. All measurement work takes expertise. It takes work to know what to do and when to do it so that the data is repeatable, reliable and accurate. Otherwise the data collection process is a waste of resources and the analysis will be misleading.

- This type of work is subject to the conditions and state of mind of the Attendee. Since they know they are being asked questions the Observer effect comes into play. What they say may or may not be true from person to person and from question to question. For an Exhibitor the core interest is in understanding and accounting for variation in behavior within a particular Attendee group and between groups (or even shows). Developing reliable measures of an Attendee's consumption based on: self-reporting, rankings by subject matter experts; ratings by objective outsiders, the use of formal data and information, and type or choices in experimental methods requires expertise. After all, the true test of a theoretical concept or postulate is only as good as the measurement system.

- This type of data takes a sample of the whole population because the cost of sampling everyone is typically too high. The three main advantages of sampling the population are that; the cost is lower, data collection can be faster, and since the data set is smaller it is typically less complicated to improve the accuracy and quality of the data.

6. Lead and registration data is gathered at trade shows but typically not gathered at Consumer events. The information obtained during the registration process can really give great insight into the subculture of the show and the demographic breakdown. Lead data has historically proven to be unreliable in terms of the time and date stamps of the lead swipes because the equipment will arrive from different shows and areas of the country. Unfortunately, none of the lead companies have good standard operating procedures (SOP's) with regards to synchronizing the lead devices. Buying-BehaviorMETRICS was the first company that attempted to use the lead data to track individuals in correlation to video footage only to discover that the synchronizing issue is a show stopper. The fact that the lead companies have also gone into the RFID business is a great concern to the integrity of this data stream as they have yet to prove their measurement systems are repeatable, reliable and statistically valid. (Verify that the lead/reg./RFID provider has synchronized these lead machines or other data capture mechanisms prior to the show starting.) Until they get more scientific and use a solid methodology like LSS with SOP's, the data will continue to be inaccurate, unreliable and misleading. Be careful with all of these data streams.

Q-maps

Just like the Implement phase Exhibitors should again add to the question map. Ask questions like:

- Who collected the data?
- How was the data collected?
- When was the data collected?
- Where was the data collected?
- Where do we get it? How is it delivered?
- What other data can be collected with it?
- What questions am I trying to answer?
- What data is needed in order to answer these questions?
- When is the data available? Who will obtain the data? How?
- What do these values represent?
- If the data is computed values, how were the values computed from the raw inputs – has there been a change in the formula over time?
- What assumptions have been made in measuring the data?
- How repeatable is the measurement of the same group in the same show?
- What level of error exists in the measurement system?
- What is the resolution of the measurement system?
- Is the measurement system accurate? Repeatable? Reliable?
- Is it acceptable across the full range of measurements needed?

Measurement Systems Evaluation (MSE)

In the LSS Exhibitor world there is a process for producing a Purchase Experience that Target Attendees (TA) find satisfying. One element of this process is face-to-face interaction between TA's and staff members. Unfortunately this process can vary dramatically from staff person to staff person based on how their different levels of experience, their skill sets even how they feel from one minute to the next. The variability in human attitudes and behaviors can create large variation in the experience process for TA's.

Just as processes like this can vary, the process of obtaining measurements and data may have variation as well. If the Exhibitor is not careful, these variations can cause defects which roll down into the Analysis phase through the Improve phase and end up as changes in the booth. A Measurement Systems Evaluation (MSE) reviews the test method, measuring instruments, and the entire process to ensure the integrity of information and data used for the Analysis phase. Data should never be accepted without a thorough understanding of the reliability of the systems that were used to collect it. MSE is an important element of Lean Six Sigma methodology because it ensures that the data collected is trustworthy and useful for driving good decisions.

MSE analyzes the collection of equipment, operations, procedures, software and personnel that affects the assignment of a number to a measurement characteristic. A MSE considers the following:

- Selecting the correct measurement and approach
- Assessing the measuring device
- Reviewing procedures & operators (SOP's)
- Verifying any measurement interactions
- Calculating the measurement uncertainty of individual measurement devices and/or measurement systems

When looking at measurement data the LSS Exhibitor asks:

- Is the data RELIABLE? - does it seem trustworthy? Is the process for measuring the data operationally standardized? Can these numbers be taken to the bank?

- Is the data REPEATABLE? - imagine asking a staff member to count the amount of money taken in at a given event. If the staff person is then asked to double check by recounting the Exhibitor would expect the measurement to be the same. If not either the staff member would recount again (repeat) or a different staff person would be asked to count (replicate) the money. Good measurement systems must be repeatable over time?

- Is the data STABLE? - is there consistency in the data? Does it seem like it is systematic or is it erratic and all over the place? Do the measurements seem to be chaotic or quotidian and commonplace?

- Is the data VALID? - would an Exhibitor be willing to stake their job on it? Does it seem creditable? Is the data on the level or does it feel like maybe you've been had? Is it too good to be true? Does it measure the theoretical concept it was designed to measure?

- Is the data ADEQUATE? - Is it sufficient evidence to overturn current thinking. To break away from "tribal ways" and tribal thinking?

How these questions are answered is the key to the analysis of this data which ultimately drives decisions down the road. Garbage in means garbage out! Consequently, making sure that good measurements are taken is very important to the improvement process. At a fundamental level data collection systems must be accurate, precise and repeatable. These are the three most important things to a measurement system.

Data collected correctly can be used to;
- make better decisions
- meet Attendee CTQ's
- achieve short/long term goals and objectives
- learn about the process and how to improve it
- understand Attendee consumption
- improve the Purchase Experience for Attendees and staff
- match the culture of the Exhibitor with the Target Attendee
- compare measurement error to specifications

Before Exhibitors can improve the booth they must listen to the voice of the system (the voice of the process). This allows them to understand the relationship between the inputs and the outputs. Once they understand the relationship they must be able to change the process inputs to get their desired results which can only be achieved through hard work in an environment where continual improvement is governed by a Lean Six Sigma methodology and culture. A culture which allows change.

When evaluating measurement systems the LSS Exhibitor should take the perspective of a detective who observes and carefully records four important aspects:

1. what changed between samples - suppose you are measuring the traffic at a 3 day show and you notice that the traffic is heavier on day 2 than on day 1 or 3. The activities surrounding day 2 of the

show would be an example of something changing between sample. The changes could be the result of some special cause event such as a storm that shut down the airports or it could be something common cause to the show such as Saturday being a busier day than Friday for a consumer show.

2. what stayed the same between samples - if you are exhibiting at a health care show and the Attendees are all Radiologists the variation in the Attendee from day to day would be minimal. The type of Attendee and their interests would stay the same from day to day.

3. what changed within the samples - suppose that you are exhibiting at the CIFES which has themed days. On day 1 they have dairy day which is geared towards dairy farmers, day 2 is livestock day for farmers who raise cattle and other animals and day 3 is produce day for growers of fruits, vegetables and grains. The offerings that each Attendee would be interested in (even their CTQ's) would most likely be different because the type of Attendee is changing over (within the 3 day show sample) the course of the show.

4. what stayed the same within the samples - similar to the second example if you are measuring the booth looking at the variation across a day, the booth staff and properties will typically be the same within the sample day.

Good analysis can not be done unless the measurement system is reliable, repeatable, stable, valid and adequate. With these things in mind the measurement system should be evaluated for:

- Accuracy - the accuracy of a measurement system is the degree of closeness of measurements of a quantity to that quantity's actual (true) value. (This is akin to hitting the bull's eye in archery.)

- Precision - The precision of a measurement system is the degree to which repeated measurements under unchanged conditions show the same results. (This is akin to grouping multiple arrows together.)

1. Accurate but not precise

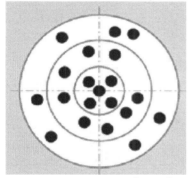

Low Cp & High Cpk

2. Not accurate and not precise

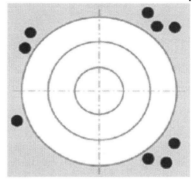

Low Cp & Low Cpk

3. Precise but not accurate

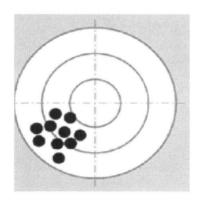

High Cp & Low Cpk

4. Accurate and Precise

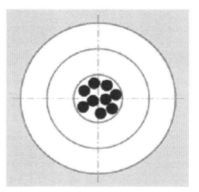

High Cp & High Cpk

- In figure 1 the shots are scattered throughout the target area but are distributed around the center or mean.
- In figure 2 the shots are unevenly grouped and outside the target area.
- In figure 3 the shots are grouped together nicely but not centered on the target. Shifting the mean to the center of the target is the next step in improvement.
- In figure 4 the shots are nicely grouped together with very little variation between shots and they are also centered on the target.

A measurement system can be accurate but not precise, precise but not accurate, neither, or both. For example, while doing some work for the Chicago Auto Show (CATA) they submitted some data on the number of Attendees entering the show. The had sold over 80,000 tickets on-site and another 40,000 on-line so they hired GES to do some traffic analysis for them. GES reported that they had counted approximately 60,000 people entering the floor. CATA didn't tell GES how many tickets they had sold. Instead they asked them to recount the data because it did not seem very accurate. At a minimum they were expecting at least as many Attendees as tickets sold. After all, why would Attendees purchase a ticket and then leave without entering the show? GES returned and reported back with a recount of about 50,000 people which they felt was very close to their original number. Both of their counts were within 10,000 of each other which GES felt was great (which it wasn't). What they didn't realize was that although their numbers were somewhat precise they were not accurate and in fact the numbers were getting less accurate. The end result was that CATA was stuck with inaccurate data from the flawed GES measurement systems.

For a measurement system to be designated as LSS it must be accurate, precise, reliable and repeatable. It must be able to distinguish one data point from another at an appropriate level of discernment to answer the question being asked. Meaning a person traveling from Chicago to Boston who wants to know how far apart the two cities are would appropriately measure the trip in miles not inches. The level of discrimination makes the measurement useful and informative relative to the question. Other elements of a measurement system which must be considered are;

- Reproducibility - refers to the ability of staff members or measurement devices to get the same average measurements time after time. We will often run the same piece of video through our automated measurement systems multiple times to verify that the same counts are obtained each time.
- Replicated - refers to the ability of the same or similar measurements to be obtained by different systems or even individuals. For example we often have different operators measure the same piece of video to verify that they measurements taken are precise and accurate.
- Staff Bias effects - different staff members get detectably different measurements and averages for the same information. We typically have four different people measure the same segment of video and we compare the numbers that each person gets in order to verify that there are not differences. If one person is consistently coming up with radically different numbers than the others we evaluate what they are doing and how they are doing it.
- Equipment bias: different devices get detectably different averages of the same measurement segments. Sometimes the software or equipment can have glitches or miscues which create anomalies in the data such as the time stamp being out of synch on lead devices.

In Control/Out of Control - Special/Common Cause

In Control versus Out of Control - In the LSS world control charts of data are often made to determine if a system is "in or out of control". Suppose you are a company that sells gift items at shows. If the number of sales per day over the course of a 12 day consumer gift show were put on a graph and the chart showed that for eleven of the twelve days you sold between 80 and 100 items but on one of the days you sold only 2 items you would speculate that something must have been different on that one day. A chart of this data would show the range of the data between 80 and 100 with one data point that was way below the range of the other points. This one point which is out of control stands out like a sore thumb and would move the Exhibitor to ask "what caused this one point to be so far out of whack?" In later phases how to analyze data like this will be explained in order to determine if the point was the result of;

- a special event (special cause) such as when there was an ice storm on a show day and the show was closed due to a power outage, (incidentally this happened to one of my Customers last year and they were furious at the staff for not delivering until they learned about this special cause).

- a common cause activity which is normal to the show. Staff will often get less efficient as the day or show goes on. The show starts off full of pep and energy but as the days go on the energy diminishes. As the energy dissipates the staff senses it (due to reference experience effect) and slows down as well. This results in less interaction and lower conversion rates. This is a common cause problem and therefore requires common cause action (training/more breaks).

- an error in the measurement system. If the measurement variation overshadows the process variation any improvements to the process will be undetectable due to the extreme measurement error. If the lead swipe machine is out of synch and showing the wrong time of capture. No amount of improvement to the lead gathering process will be detectable.

Stability The ability of the measurement process to maintain precision, accuracy, and repeatability over time. If different staff members measure the number of engagements with a display they get about the same answer. If we move the display and remeasure the same display 10 times we may see a shift in the average number of engagements. However, the range of the readings from the two staff people should be about the same. If not this is a stability issue.

Specifications

Measurement activity requires the creation of specifications (targets) and in order to ensure accurate collection of information and data. Specifications are another means to hear the voice of the customer but not the voice of the process. Meaning the number of sales is an indicator that an Exhibitor has the right product, in the right place at the right price for their Customers. It doesn't tell them that their distribution process is working efficiently. So comparing sales numbers to targets or specifications will not lead to improvement of the distribution process. Similarly comparing the number of leads to an arbitrary target number will not improve the quality of the leads gathered. The specification approach does not reveal any insights into how the process works. That said there are different types of specifications which should be developed.

First there are specifications which are facts based. A specification qualifies as facts based if it has been proven true over time by data and information rather than somebody's opinion or tribal knowledge. For example knowing that 20% of the Attendees at the RSNA are interested in INFORAD it would be appropriate to set specifications to draw in 20% of the Attendees at the show. The time proven facts based data showing that only 20% are interested in this venue makes the specification meaningful.

Next there are specifications which are plan based. Estimates, forecasts and budgets would typically fall in this category. These are based upon analysis of past data, present day activities and future projections. These predictions should not be taken as targets but typically are. Projecting data from the past into the future for the purpose of setting goals is not very helpful especially when conditions change so dramatically as they have during this recent recession. Very few if any Exhibitors forecasted this recession and/or how deep it has been. It would be insane to expect anyone to perform up to forecasted target levels under the recessionary conditions but many Exhibit Managers heads have rolled due to under performance. Predictions should be used for guidance and help instead of judgment and blame.

Finally, there are specifications which are randomly assessed targets. While the values in the first two categories are often helpful or even necessary, arbitrary numerical targets are neither. In fact they are often detrimental. When the specification value is fact based, or planning based it is useful to know how the current values compare to the specifications because it is an indicator of the Attendees behavior and consumption. When the specification is an arbitrary numerical goal, then it can be very dangerous to make that same comparison. For example, consider an arbitrary lead swipe target. If a particular show's value is above target, the management may be tempted to assume that the show spending was worthwhile and should be increased. If this show's value is low, then they may be tempted to cut spending to the show. With this in mind Exhibit Managers are incented to either get as few leads as possible (if they don't want to do the show anymore) or to get as many leads as possible regardless of the quality of the leads. Which means they swipe no one or they swipe everyone.

In either case the activity generated is based on hitting the target number of lead swipes. Shows can be eliminated or incorporated, staff can be fired and hired, money can be spent, and all because the Exhibit Manager does or doesn't satisfactorily explain, show after show, why the shows have or have not met the lead quota. When Exhibitors are pressured to meet a goal or to hit a target value such as getting a specific number of leads, there are three ways they can achieve their goal or hit their specification.

1. They can work to improve the system
2. They can cheat, manipulate and distort the process or system
3. They can cheat, manipulate and distort the data

You can make data say anything you want by changing the way you sample the data and/or the way you act in the booth. The size of the sampling and/or subgrouping will skew the analysis in the same way that yelling at the staff to swipe more leads will get you more leads. Things that may be significant on paper may not be the most significant in the Purchase Experience environment. Always question the data. What does it really mean? Is the data telling us something or only acting as if it is telling us something? Are we setting a target number or specification arbitrarily? Is this target encouraging change and learnings and are we driving continuous improvement?

If an Exhibitor can only COMPARE data to the targets, but they are unable to improve the system, they are left with only the last two ways of meeting their goals (they get the staff to swipe everyone or they just report a higher number of leads). When a current value is compared to an arbitrary numerical target, the business which is a consequence of the specification approach, will tempt the Exhibit Manager and staff to make the data look favorable. Unfortunately it is always easier to manipulate or distort the data than to improve the system. Consequently, the number of leads increases but the leads are not qualified or useful.

Attaining a target goal will tell you where you are but it will not tell an Exhibitor how they got there. If it continues from show to show they will get deeper into the quagmire and it will not tell them how to get out of the mess they get stuck in. When targets or specifications like budgets, goals, plans, forecasts or objectives are arbitrary they create tension in the organization. The adherence to hitting them will drive either apathy and neglect or intense stress and panic. The culture will become passive and withdrawn or hostile and aggressive in order to alleviate the tension. Either way the process or data or both will be distorted and defective. The Purchase Experience will not improve and the Attendees will eventually stop coming.

Standard Operating Procedure (SOP)

An SOP is a document that specifies how the data is to be captured in a systematic, consistent manner. LSS Exhibitors develop SOP's for the capture and measurement of data to ensure that it is executed consistently. The SOP should list:
- the goals for measurement
- the questions being answered

- the document or mechanism for data capture
- definitions of any terms that are applicable
- and the process that should be adhered to in execution of the measurement

Here is an example of an SOP document.

Document 610-C
Main Booth Traffic

Goal of the measurement: Defines Attraction, Interaction, In booth interaction, Engagement, and In booth engagement rates.

Questions being answered:
1. How many people pass-by the booth?
2. How many people stop-by the booth?
3. How many people interact with the booth staff?
4. How many people engage with the presentation, products, demos, flyers, etc.?

Documentation used: Booth Traffic Template

Definitions:
- Pass-by traffic –Attendees that passed by the area and therefore have an awareness of it but do not stop-by, engage or interact.
- Stop-by traffic-Attendees that are attracted enough to the area to enter the booth.
- Engagement traffic-Attendees that engage with; a display, attend a

presentation, a hands on demonstration, touch a product...Etc. (perform consideration activities)

- Interaction traffic-Attendees that display enough of a preference to interact with the booth staff face-to-face.
- Attraction Rate (AR): number of people that stop-by the booth versus pass-by the booth(AR = total Stop-bys/total pass-bys)
- Engagement Rate(ER): number of engagements versus number of people who pass-by and stop-by (ER = total Engagement/(total pass-by + total stop-by)
- In-booth Engagement Rate (IER): number of engagement versus number of people who stop-by (IER = total engagement/total stop-by)
- Interaction Rate (IR): number of interactions versus number of people who pass-by and stop-by (IR = total interaction/(total pass-by + total stop-by)
- In booth Interaction Rate (IER): number of interactions versus number of people who stop-by (IER = total interaction/total stop-by)

Process:

1. Watch video and count how many attendees per 15 minute clip pass-by the booth, stop-by the booth, interact with the booth staff, and / or engagement with booth properties. You will continue doing this for the remainder of the day.

2. Input the results into the Booth Traffic template

3. Verify that the measurements are correctly entered into the template.

4. Verify that the rate formulas are correctly calculating the rates.

5. Create a Power Point slide with the Excel graph from the template.

At its heart, Lean Six Sigma is data driven and has its base in statistics. Therefore, the key to any successful Lean Six Sigma measurement phase is data that is; reliable, repeatable, stable, valid and adequate. The steps taken to capturing good data cannot be skipped or shortened.

Data Tracking Sheet (DTS)

The tool which is used to document the capture of the measurement information and data is the Data Tracking Sheet (DTS). The goal of this document is to record the status and progress of the measurement activity going on during the Measure Phase. There are different sources of measurement and tracking them will allow the Exhibitor to quickly assess the timeline, resource allocation and update the Gantt for communication to all process partners in the project.

Sample Data Tracking Sheet							
Description	Data Source	Person Responsible	Day 1 of the show	Day 2 of the show	Question being Answered	Capture Document Used
booth entrance	Camera 1	Genna Grenade	9am-5pm	Not applicable	How many TA's enter the booth?	627-B Entrance Metrics
Presentation	Hand Camera	Ellie Painter	N/A	10:00 am	What is the drop-out rate?	749-A Drop-out Metrics

The DTS keeps the project moving forward, records the where data was obtained and relates the data to questions being asked. This documentation is especially useful as teams repeat the DIMAIC cycle and implement experimental changes to the booth from show to show or year to year. Even if team members come and go the new staff can keep the measurement systems and sources consistent as they gather the data.

Listed on the DTS per the example on the previous page is the description of the measurement being taken (e.g. the entrance to the booth) followed by a description of the data source (video from camera #1) which links back to the DCP (Data Capture Plan) . Next is the name of the person responsible for measuring this item or collecting this information. The next two boxes are indicators of which show days the data is applicable for. For example Exhibitors might have a live presentation on day 2 of the show and they are measuring the number of people in the presentation on day 2. This measurement is not applicable to the other days of the show. (note that the example only shows two days but there should be as many columns as there are show days.) The next column indicates the question that this measurement is attempting to address. Questions lead and answers follow so it is very important to match the question with the metrics. Finally, when doing this activity show after show it is a good idea to have some SOP or standardized document to capture the data on. This will become particularly valuable when you get to the Analysis phase.

Run Charts and Control Charts

Another tool that LSS Exhibitors use often to capture and later analyze information and data are the run chart and the control chart. Measurements reveal how much variation there is in a system, process or population and graphical representations allow the Exhibitor to see and differentiate the variation. A metric that is "in control" implies a stable, predictable, amount of variation due mainly to common causes where a metric that is "out of control" implies an unstable, unpredictable amount of variation. This variation is due to special and/or common causes.

Run Charts and Control Charts are used;
- as a means to monitor process variables (x's) and resultants (Y's). The intent is to assess the stability of a measured resultant (Y) and to "flag" when a process goes out-of-control.
- as a means to validate the effect of changes on either Y's or y's. Control charts can be used to assess the effectiveness of changes made to products or processes.
- to understand the stability and variation in critical x's identified using designed experiments (DOE's).
- for follow-up studies of factors after DOE's have been run (critical x's)

When charting the outputs (Y's), Exhibitors sometimes find they are monitoring or controlling the wrong things and that we really need to examine the x's. they need to look at the process and then look at it again later. If the change looks greater between the two times they looked than within the times they looked then the factors controlled within the booth are not as important as the factors at work in the background of the show. If the change within the look is greater than between looks then they have the more significant factors in the booth. If run and control charts don't give the Exhibitor what they are looking for, then they are not looking at the right thing.

Building a Run Chart and Control Chart
1. Collect the data
2. Create a graph with a vertical line (y-axis) scale related to the measurement and the horizontal line (x-axis) as a time scale.

3. Place the measurements on the chart in time order
4. Calculate the median (average) and draw a horizontal line across the median
5. Calculate the upper (UCL) and lower (LCL) control limits

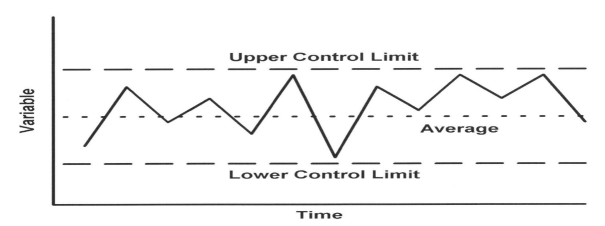

Control charts are used to monitor a process. By measuring variables (x's), parameters (y's) it's easy to assess the stability of a measured resultants (Y) and identify when a process goes out-of-control. Control charts can be used to validate the effect of changes on either Y's or y's. Thus Exhibitors can use control charts as a way to assess the effectiveness of changes made to the booth and their impact on the Purchase Experience. The control chart is a little bit more complicated than a run chart because it has two components the individual chart and the moving range chart. To create a control chart the upper and lower control limits the range and standard deviation are needed.

Calculations of individual's chart
1. determine sampling plan
2. take a sample at each specified interval of time
3. calculate the moving range for the sample

4. plot the data (individual and moving range)
5. after sufficient x's and noise have been captured (# observations required) use software to calculate the control limits for moving range chart

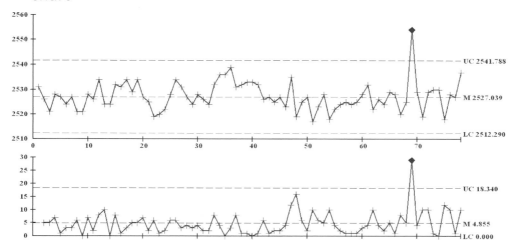

Sample control chart - notice the dramatic spike at point 70 during the "show special" promotion. Clearly this shows that the promotion moved the needle on sales revenue.

When considering control chart variation:

- If the range chart is not in control, take appropriate action (special cause action for special causes, common cause action for common causes)
- If the range chart is in control calculate the limits for individual chart
- If the individuals chart is not in control, take appropriate action (special cause action for special causes, common cause action for common causes)
- If the individuals chart is in control carefully and critically examine your sampling strategy. Determine whether appropriate variation

is being captured in your sampling scheme. Consider changing the sampling and subgrouping plans, or designing an experiment to move the average of the individual chart or reduce the range of variation.

Process Sigma

The product isn't just what the Attendee takes with him or her as they walk out of the booth, it is also what and how the Attendee feels about the Purchase Experience and the Exhibitors offering. In order to start identifying errors, mistakes and defects which prevent the Purchase Experience from being something wonderful for your Target Attendees, Exhibitors need to understand the needs of TA's. The VOC plan can be used to gather Attendee insights/information/comments/quotes/issues and transform them into specifications. The feedback captured should help to generate the Critical To Quality (CTQ) characteristics which the product or service offering must meet in order to deliver a satisfying Purchase Experience. The ability of the offering to meet these CTQ requirements without a defect or error can be quantified as an Exhibitor "process sigma" which is a calculation based on the number of failures (defects) in relation to the number of opportunities for success. A Lean Six Sigma level of quality is such that out of a million opportunities to succeed by delivering a satisfying Purchase Experience to the Attendee or Customer the process only fails (produces a defect) 3.4 times.

A defect is defined as anytime the Purchase Experience does not meet these CTQ requirements, does not meet Attendee specifications, causes Customer dissatisfaction, or does not fulfill the functional or physical requirements of the Customer (TA). The term Customer refers to both internal and external customers. e.g. the situation where only 30% of Attendees having face-to-face interactions with staff would be a 70% defect rate for an external Customer. This can be compared to the situation where an Executive (internal Customer) requires that the booth highlights the companies "innovation". Typically both the external Attendee and the internal executives CTQ requirements must be successfully met at the minimum defect level in order for the event to be deemed "successful".

Opportunities are the total number of chances to please the Customer. These chances must be independent of each other and must be repeatably and accurately measurable and Customer CTQ driven. By comparing the number of opportunities handled successfully against the number that have defects the Exhibitor can calculate their overall process sigma as well as their process sigma from event to event. Over time this metric can serve as a capability metric which can be used consistently to determine what is and is not working in the booth.

Calculating Process Sigma

Step 1: Establish the number of potential opportunities (X_1)
Although this could differ based on the phase of the Purchase Experience process and the Customer the Exhibitor is focusing on here are some typical scenarios;

- At the Awareness phase the potential opportunities would mean the number of Target Attendees (in relationship to the total number of Attendees) who pass-by the booth. So if the Exhibitor knows that 80% of the Attendees at the show are potential buyers of the offering (Target Attendees) and the goal is to make them aware of the offering by seeing it in the booth. An Exhibitor could count the number of Attendees per hour who pass the booth and view the offering.

- At the Consideration phase the Exhibitor would count the number of Attendees who stop-by the booth and see the booth presentation.

- At the Preference phase they would count the number of Attendees who have an interaction with a booth staff person in a hands-on demonstration.

- At the Conversion phase the Exhibitor would measure the number of sales made.

Step 2: Determine the level of Defects (X_2)

This is an inability to meet a Customer CTQ so as before this could differ by phase so to stay consistent with the opportunities it is typically things like;

- At the Awareness phase a defect could mean the number of Target Attendees in relationship to the total number of Attendees who never pass-by the booth. So if the Exhibitor knows that 80% of the Attendees at the show are potential buyers of the offering (Target Attendees) and their goal is to make TA's aware of the offering by seeing it in the booth. An Exhibitor could count the number of Attendees who never pass the booth and/or view the booth. This could also be a metric like the number who do not recall having seen the booth or do not see the message.

- At the Consideration phase the Exhibitor might count the number of Attendees who do not stop-by the booth to engage with the booth properties. e.g. if 100 Attendees pass-by the booth and 20 stop-by the booth the defect would be 80 Attendees who were not attracted to the booth.

- At the Preference phase they could count the number of Attendees who do not have an interaction with a booth staff person in a hands-on demonstration. If 20 Attendees stop-by the booth but only 5 interact with a staff person there would be 15 defects.

- At the Conversion phase the Exhibitor could measure the number of Attendees who leave the booth without making a purchase or swiping a lead.

Step 3: After Implementation Measure the Opportunities and Defects
Once the Exhibitor has established what the opportunities and defects are they can implement the exhibit and measure them. At the show they can execute a measurement plan and collect data that is repeatable, reliable, accurate, precise and statistically valid.

Step 4: Calculate your Process Yield (Py)
By subtracting the total number of defects from the total number of opportunities, dividing by the total number of opportunities, and finally multiplying the result by 100.

$$((Opportunities-Defects)/Opportunities) * 100 = Process\ Yield$$

$$((X_1-X_2)/X_1) * 100 = Py$$

Step 5: Assess your Process Sigma Tabulation
Take your Process Yield (Py) value and look up your sigma on a sigma conversion table. The following is a (shortened) sigma conversion table.

Defects per Million Opportunities	Sigma Level	Process Yield Py
933193	0.00	6.700000
841300	0.500	15.900000
691462	**1.000**	**30.900000**
500000	1.500	50.000000
308538	2.000	69.100000
158655	2.500	84.100000
66807	3.000	93.300000
10724	3.80	98.900000
6210	4.00	99.400000
1350	4.50	99.870000
233	5.00	99.980000
32	5.50	99.996800
2	6.00	99.999660

Sample Calculation

So now that you have seen how to calculate a process sigma let's end the Measure phase by doing a sample calculation as preparation for the Analysis phase.
- Select the important measure(s) for the booth
- Determine the capabilities of the measurement system (MSE)
- Describe/display the variation with graphs and tables
- Calculate the sigma level

Suppose an Exhibitor set up their booth at the next show knowing they are at the conversion phase. Success for them at the conversion phase is swiping a lead in order to follow-up with the Target Attendee after the show. They also know that 40% of the Attendees at the show meet their Target Attendee criteria.

The show opens and the Exhibitor sets up cameras and measures 500 people per hour pass-by the booth for a total of 4000 Attendees over the 8 hours of the show. Of the 4000 who pass-by 3200 (80%) enter the booth. Wow that is outstanding success and it means they are doing an excellent job of attracting their Target Attendee. It also means they have a lot of opportunity for leads. However, in order to convert them successfully they must interact with TA's face-to-face. The measurement shows that they only interacted with 960 (30% of the opportunities) of these Target Attendees. So what is their process sigma?

$$((\text{Opportunities-Defects})/\text{Opportunities}) * 100 = \text{Process Yield}$$
$$((X_1-X_2)/X_1) * 100 = Py$$

There were 960 successes (interactions) which means there were
$$(3200-960)=2240 \text{ defects (non-interactions)}$$
$$((3200-2240)/3200)*100 = 30$$

Per the table a process yield corresponds roughly with **691462** per million opportunities and a process sigma of about 1. For this Exhibitor there is a lot of work to do to get down to only 3.4 missed interactions per million Target Attendees in the booth. They are a long way from being a Lean Six Sigma Exhibitor. However think of the potential for improvement. They are only interacting with 30% of the Attendees. An average sale generates $5000 dollars and they close 10% of the leads they generate at the show. If they double or even triple their interaction rate they would be at 2 sigma and their sales would increase by $960,000 dollars. That would definitely be a project worth doing and if they could simultaneously improve their close rate it would drive the ROI even higher. So it is clear to see that calculating a process sigma allows the Exhibitor to draw a line in the sand to use as a measuring reference point for continuous improvement.

This situation is common in the Exhibitor world due largely to the fact that Exhibitors do not adhere to a methodology that is striving toward continuous improvement. Lean Six Sigma provides the platform to drive change that cycles of improvement. By obtaining good metrics during the Measure phase an Exhibitor can confidently move into the Analyze phase and get to the root causes of defects and errors.

Chapter 5

Analyze Phase

Mona Lisas and Mad Hatters

For unless they see the sky.....
they know not if it's dark outside or light.
Elton John

At the Analyze phase there are a few fundamental elements that must be in place in order to be a Lean Six Sigma Exhibitor. Analysis is only as good as the measurement data and input information that goes into it. Garbage in means garbage out. The data collection process needs a solid methodology. One of the LSS sayings is "No matter what the data, and no matter how the values are arranged and presented, one must always use some method of analysis to come up with an interpretation of the data" - unknown.

The good news is that you don't have to have a PhD. in statistics to do great analysis work. Now-a-days software is so savvy it can take the data and perform every kind of number crunching you can imagine and much, much more than you will ever need. But the software is only part of the story. There is also the information available on the internet.

This morning, I googled t-test (a type of significance test you will learn about in this chapter) and google returned 236,000,000 results. WOW! You don't need to know how to calculate a t-test (and if you do want to know, there are 236M places to look on the internet) but you should learn how to interpret the results to drive better experiments and decisions. So that is what I will focus on. In addition I will put some helpful hints on how to do some of the calculations on our website www.bbmgo.com.

The Starting Point

As a starting point analysis methodology needs more than experience as a foundation or the interpretation will only be as good as the Exhibitor's past experience. There are a lot of Exhibitors who have years of solid experience and there are a lot who have one year of weak experience which they repeat over and over again. Humans emulate success and repeat their behaviors based on previous successes. Many managers fly by the seat of their pants and make decisions based on their experience but leave a wake of problems for the workers in the organization. Exhibitors tend to copy what other Exhibitors do without reviewing data or understanding the impact of the choices they make until it is too late.

Data should be viewed in context. I remember a conversation with my nephew regarding an article in the paper that said 1 out of every 4 kids has regular sexual activity while in high school. My nephew was shocked and said he didn't know a single kid who had "regular sexual activity". In the city of Benton Harbor which is across the rive from where I live, more than half of the boys (58%) drop out of high school. To take that data out of context and assume that our national school system is failing would be irresponsible. These types of examples reinforce the concept that data must be kept in context or it will lead to bad analysis and bad decisions.

The analysis must use data to drive good Attendee (Customer) driven decisions. When management is making decisions without specific Attendee focused data to support their decisions it is a red flag. The old expression "in God we trust all others bring data" has meaning for an LSS Exhibitor. Customer focused data means that the data is not based on arbitrary target numbers as data is in most monthly reports. *"Managing a company by means of the monthly report is like trying to drive a car by watching the yellow line in the rear-view mirror"*-Myron Tribus

In a typical monthly management report each line;
- Gives the current value
- Lists a plan or average value
- Compares the current value to this plan or average value

- Compares the current value to the value for the same month last year
- Gives the current year-to-date cumulative value
- Compares this year-to-date value with a plan or average value
- Compares the current and previous year-to-date values

All of these metrics are rear view mirror in nature and single point oriented. There is no graphical component to most management reports and no continuous stream of points, only this point compared to another point. With this point mentality it is not possible to see trends or patterns in the data which makes it even less likely that predictions can be defined accurately. In short these types of reports make it difficult to take appropriate actions because good decision making starts with asking the right questions, capturing Attendee focused data and analysis driven by a sound methodology based on;

1. Identifying possible causes
2. Narrowing down to root causes
3. Brainstorming ways to improve it
4. Quantifying the fix
5. Assessing the feasibility of the change
6. Executing the improvement

The LSS analysis approach has three segments which must always be followed in order;

1. Practical - when looking at the data ask "does this look realistic? Based on knowledge of the subject matter does this seem reasonable? Does this make sense?" Cognitive skills should work together to keep the data in context. Never trust any data that is not in context and don't trust anyone who will not provide context for their

figures. If people have done the work they love to show it off, if they haven't they will hem and haw.

2. Graphical - Numerical summaries are good but they are no substitute for graphs. Make graphs, plots and charts of the data in every way you can because pictures make the numbers more accessible to the human mind. A picture is worth a thousand words and visualizing the data can often make the analysis obvious. Trends and patterns can be identified and it is one of the best ways to communicate with team members. Making graphs, charts and plots will allow you to keep values in context. No data has value apart from its' context.

3. Analytical - run the data through a series of statistical test against hypothesis to verify the relevance of the data. Software today is sophisticated enough that you can run data through a myriad of statistical evaluations with the click of a mouse. You don't need to know the formulas and math behind it (don't get me wrong it is a good idea to know the math especially at the Black Belt level and above but a lot can be done with a click) and most (including Excel) have more tools than you will ever use. Don't allow the data reporting to become a comparison of two values unless it is a broad generalization not meant for decision making.

At the Orange Belt level there are a lot of tools that are common to the Analysis phase including: Pareto charts, run charts, control charts, calibration studies, components of variance (COV), Attribute Studies, ANOVA and others. The tool selected is usually determined by characteristics of the measurement system itself and the question being asked. So let's briefly revisit some of the questions that should be added to the Q-map.

Q-map- [questions lead and answers follow]

At this phase it is necessary to ask the why questions. In order to drive solutions during the Improve phase. Questions to ask when analyzing data:

- Why hasn't this problem/issue been fixed before?
- What, historically, has been the problem (center or variation)?
- How does the statement of the problem affect the analysis and experiment strategy?
- How should the data be organized to meet the objectives?
- What analysis should we run to verify our CTQ's?
- How might these assumptions affect our conclusions?
- What else could be analyzed from the show?
- What are the effects of the factors and the relationships between them?
- What conclusions could be made?
- What is changing within the show? What is changing between groups? Why is or isn't it changing?
- What trends or patterns are visible in the data?
- How much within show variation do we have? Why?
- What assumptions have been made in running the data? Why?
- Does the data even make sense? Why or why not?
- What restrictions are there about the data and analysis of it? Why?
- Is the data adequate? Why or why not?
- How was the data collected? Why was it collected in this manner?
- What comments can be made about the response variable?
- What observations can be made about the data?
- How does the analysis compare with our predictions?
- How well do we understand what is CTQ for our Target Attendees?
- What factors may have influenced the results? Why?

Pareto Charts

Pareto charts are based on the Pareto principle which states that there are a "vital few" number of critical elements (factors) of any significant event and these elements should be addressed first (high priority). How we evaluate what is "critical" is the key to prioritizing. In the Exhibitor world the show opens and the show closes. During the time surrounding that everything is seemingly critical and therefore a priority. Pareto charts help to simplify analysis so caution should be used in drawing specific conclusions. When using Pareto charts it is a good idea to make sure the critical factors identified are truly THE critical factors keeping in mind that often factors are confounded with one another. For example, the difference in the color of carpeting between the booth carpet and the aisle carpet will create a force-field effect that result in staff standing on one side and Attendees standing in the safety of the aisle. This often leads Exhibitors to believe that carpet color is critical. But the color is confounded with the behavior of the staff person. If the staff person is inviting and asks the Attendee into the booth this critical factor can be quickly neutralized because the forcefield effect is psychologically combined with the body language and approach of the staff person.

How do you create a Pareto chart?
1. Gather the data (make sure the data is valid)
2. Sort it by categories or groups
3. Make sure that the categories can not be split further
4. Arrange the categories by highest frequency (priority) in the data
5. Chart the data in order from high to low
6. Work on the problems from high to low priority

Sample Pareto Chart
Reasons Attendees Left the Booth without Interacting

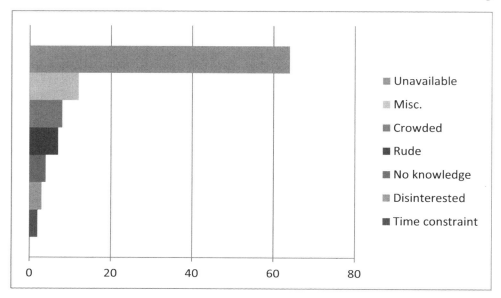

The sample Pareto chart above is a visual depiction of Attendee reasons for leaving a booth without interacting with a staff person face-to-face in a demonstration. As you can see the number one priority was related to the Attendee voice CTQ which screamed that they left because a staff person was not available. This might be due to a myriad of reasons such as; staffing issue (not enough staff people), the staff clustering together and talking to each other instead of Attendees, a lengthy demonstration process that kept the staff tied up with other Attendees...etc. Knowing that this was a critical factor driving the Attendee to leave without interacting allows the Exhibitor to focus on making staff available instead of worrying about the booth being too crowded or the staff not being knowledgeable about the offering. It also showed that low priority issues such as the Attendee being under a time crunch were not vital. This compounded with the unavailable issue indicates that the Exhibitor could be able to spend valuable time with the

Attendee if the staff members were available which would be well worth experimenting on as interplaying factors.

Value Stream Map (VSM)

In the Implement phase the ability to make a process map and flow diagram was developed. These tools will now be used in the Analyze phase for the creation of a value stream map (VSM). The VSM is a practical analysis tool that categorizes activities into three segments: value added (VA), non-value added (NVA) and necessary to quality (NTQ). Using these distinctions the Exhibitor team can collectively identify and eliminate the non-value added activities in each process step and reduce the waste in the process steps wherever possible. NTQ activities, however, cannot be totally eliminated from a system. These items are often driven by high social political capital or tribal knowledge like when an executive in the company wants something done a certain way because it has always been done that way regardless of the value. For example, many Exhibitor believed that their booth must always be the first booth in the show. In situations like this the NTQ items can be called out in hopes that the constraints of this activity are evident. In time these items will continue increasing inefficiencies and costs which could drive them to be eliminated down the road making the process leaner.

For example; In a process under study, the value stream map demonstrated that the workflow went to the same approver twice. The process steps on either side of the approval did not make any significant changes or add any value. In addition the subsequent steps were not dependent on the second approval. Hence, the second approval was eliminated because it did not add any value to the process and delayed the implementation.

Current State Map

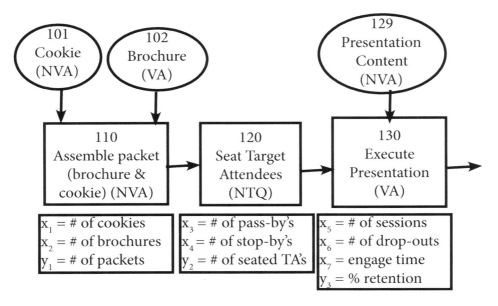

Going back to our previous example, suppose the Exhibitor discovered that Attendees did not like the cookies. This means the cookie step was NVA and subsequently the assemble packets step becomes NVA. In addition they found that hiring a presentation company to create presentation content was not a value add to the process. The time and resources required to get the company up to speed on the Company offering for development of content was so high the Exhibitor realized they were better off doing it themselves. Streamlining the process allowed them to eliminate these steps and focus their resources on other issues. It also creates a great experimental moment. So the booth was measured after the changes to verify that there were no negative impact on the Attendee Purchase Experience. The big benefit of these eliminations was that their logistical constraints went away and their costs were reduced. Eliminating items help streamline a process and reducing variation. These are common benefits for using the value stream map.

Why Tree Analysis

Another great analysis tool is the Why Tree. This is a tool that can be done by an individual or in a team setting. To start the analysis a problem statement is made using input from the VOC mechanism. For example the VOC mechanism might output a defect statement like;

67% of Attendees complained that they did not get a follow-up after the show.

Once the problem statement is made a series of related "why questions" are asked in an effort to dig down to the root cause of the problem.

Why Tree example;
1. Why weren't the Attendees called back?
The sales force did not call them.

2. Why didn't the sales force call them?
Because they did not feel the leads were valuable.

3. Why didn't they feel the leads are valuable?
Past experience has shown that the leads weren't qualified.

4. Why weren't the leads qualified
The booth staff was driven to capture a target number of leads not a number of qualified leads.

5. Why were they driven to hit a target instead of getting only qualified leads?
Management sets a target goal and incents them to hit it instead of incenting them to deliver qualified leads.

6. Why is management setting these targets?
It is the way they have always done it. (tribal)

Typically asking 5 why questions in a row will lead to the root cause of the problem and many people call this 5-why analysis. If five works great but if more are needed the Exhibitor should do as many as it takes until they get to a place where either; they don't know the answer or they have a root cause identified. It is often more helpful to put the questions in boxes and draw connecting arrows from one to the other like the abbreviated chart below. This typically works better for the Exhibitor team and is a better communication device.

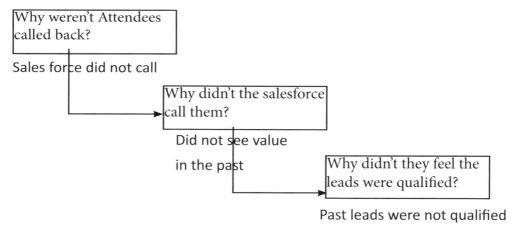

Fishbone Diagrams

A fishbone diagram is a tool that allows the team to graphically see the cause and effects relationships between elements. Often these graphical methods are helpful in driving team unity and creating an atmosphere of open idea sharing. This is vital in the getting to root causes of problems.

How to construct a fishbone diagram:

1. Start with a problem statement
2. Brainstorm for possible causes
3. Sort the possible causes into groups
4. Place the causes along the main line leading to the problem statement
5. Connect the cause boxes with lines to the main line
6. To the left of the cause box lines place possible reasons for the cause
7. To the right place possible solutions

Be careful not to be too hasty and jump to conclusions. Use data when possible to drive team decisions and measure the show before, during and after implementing the changes. Most problems have deep rooted interplay causes that are tied to other causes. Use this tool to communicate to the organization so that everyone is on-board and agrees the team has truly captured the causes and that everyone understands them well.

Problem solving is a skill set that develops with practice. Take the time to really understand the issues and the causes. If the Exhibitor does not they open the team up to the consequences of implementing a fix that doesn't work. When this happens the team can lose it's credibility and momentum. This can also make the champion look bad and that will diminish the support down the road. Use this tool to communicate a direction in an effort to increase social-political capital by avoiding political missteps.

Sample Fishbone Diagram

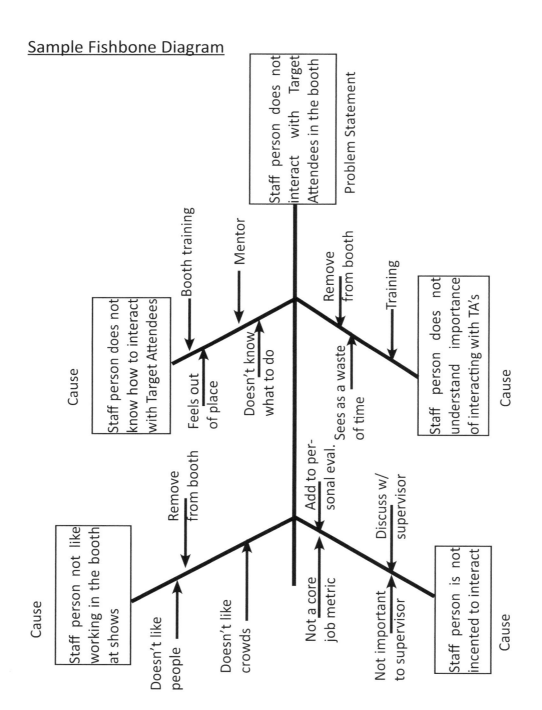

On the last page there is a sample of a fishbone diagram that has been simplified. This might be an excellent fishbone exercise to work on with the Exhibitor team as it is a common Exhibitor problem.

Line Charts-Histograms

While working at Whirlpool I was asked to give a presentation to upper management. I showed a couple of slides with some data displaying the effects of pricing factors in big box stores like Lowes and Sears. After the presentation the Vice President of Sales approached me and asked me about a graph I had shown. Oddly enough he didn't ask me about the data, he asked me what kind of chart it was. I was stunned because it was a bar chart which I thought was a pretty common item. I couldn't imaging how this guy who was an Ivy league school graduate and had worked his way through this fortune 500 company had never seen a bar chart. To this day I don't know if he was serious or not but I realized that I need to explain things even if I think they are common place especially when displaying and analyzing data.

There are a number of different plots which are used to display the same type of data with different nuances or twists. The different plotting techniques help to;

- summarize data from a process or show
- identifies the center point & the range of variation in the data
- graphically represent the data revealing the shape of the distribution
- allows for easy comparison of the data to the target/specification
- points out any irregularities or outliers in the data
- provide insight into the capability of the process in delivering a satisfactory Purchase Experience

Keys to build line charts:

1. Gather the data
2. Group the data by categories of interest
3. Tabulate the frequency of each category group
4. Make a table of the frequency data in order
5. Plot the data from the table onto a graph
6. Identify the center line and the range (spread) of the data
7. Look for patterns in the chart that indicate changes or variation in the process
8. Highlight any trends in the data and mark them on the graph

Sample Line Chart

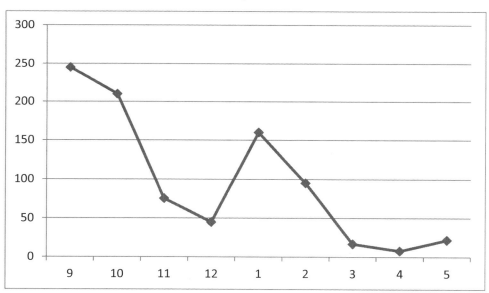

This is a line chart showing the number of Attendees per hour who engage in the booth. It is an indicator of when the booth is busy and when it is not which could be very useful for staffing the booth. This type of chart makes it easy to see trends and patterns in the data. Interestingly enough most shows are bimodal like this meaning there is a bump in traffic at the open and another bump around the lunch period when education sessions let out. Unfortunately staff members like to exit the booth at lunch time leaving the Attendees to fend for themselves. It is also worth noting that staff members will suffer from "reference experience" an effect that occurs when large traffic is followed by lower traffic and the energy level drops off. This happens because Exhibit staff feels the difference in the momentum. In the example above when we asked booth staff members how they felt at 1pm they said the booth felt dead. When we asked them how they felt about having 50 to 100 people an hour in the booth they said they would love that. Unfortunately they felt the booth was dead with this and higher volume levels because they were referencing the 250 Attendees they experienced at the opening hours. This is such a common phenomenon at shows which needs to be overcome with training.

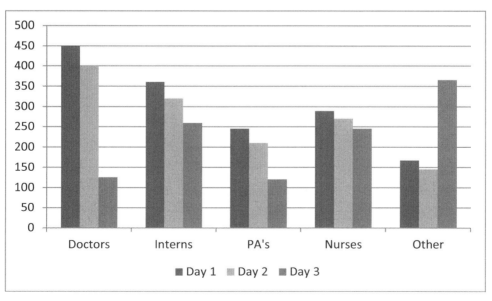

Sample of a Histogram

The previous page shows a histogram revealing the number of professionals who entered the booth by day. In this data it is interesting to note that the number of Doctors drops off by approximately 75% on Day 3, the number of PA's (physicians Assistants) also drops but only about 50%. Also note that the number of Interns and Nurses seems to stay pretty steady across all three days. Finally notice that there is a big increase in the number of "other" Attendee types who consume the booth on day 3. As it turned out this category was mainly "Hospital Administrators" who live close enough to the show to come for the day. Knowing this it might be worthwhile to stage a special activity for these Attendees especially if they are Target Attendees.

The brain is much better at processing dynamic images than long lists of numbers. Visual analytics create moments of insight for the brain that make the viewer want to learn more. When the viewers' brain can pick out size and color that makes graphs, plots and tree maps intuitive it engages and begins answering questions that the viewer didn't know he/she had. The highly engaged brain can filter through information and make discoveries on its' own. Delivering the images that get the most visceral comprehension prompts the most participation and engagement. For this reason graphical methods of presenting data are most effective.

Statistics Overview

In the Analysis Phase LSS Exhibitors are typically concerned with three major things regarding the measurements they have obtained;

- Is the data showing that the Purchase Experience process they have created is "in control" or "out of control"? If the data is plotted are there wild spike in the data which indicate that the process is out of control or are all of the points pretty much in line.

- Is the process changing within or between the parameters being analyzing. If they are looking at a show, typically Exhibitors want to know if the interaction rate is changing within a day of the show or between days of the show. They might even go bigger and examine multiple shows trying to identify if things are different within a show or between different shows. They might go even bigger and look at the things changing between/within show seasons or years.

- Finally Exhibitors want to know if the changes are due to some special thing that happened or is it common to the Exhibitor. For example, show attendance might be down because of a special cause event like September 11th or it might be due to a common cause like the decrease in buyers in the premium and incentive industry. (The industry has been shrinking for more than a decade according to Hall-Erickson Inc. and there are fewer and fewer buyers of premium and incentive products.) Another example would be traffic on a three day show tends to be lighter on day three. This variation from day 1 to day three is not due to some special activity or cause. It is common to the show and due to common cause.

When analyzing data it is essential that the LSS Exhibitor has a fundamental understanding of basic statistics. This starts with the understanding that most measurement data will be spread out across a continuum. Meaning there is a high and a low value which determines the **rang**e of the values in the measurement. The range (R) is a measure of the dispersion and is defined as the maximum value minus the minimum value. The remaining numbers which fall in between the high and low tend to be distributed centrally around the point which is known as the average or **mean**. While other measures of location and dispersion exist, the average and the range will take an Exhibitor a long way in analyzing most situations.

Variables are things that are measured, controlled, or manipulated and are called variables because their values change (vary). There are two different types of variables; *Independent variables* (customarily x's) are those that are manipulated whereas *dependent variables* (customarily y's) are only measured resultants. If every value of x is associated with a value of y, then y is said to be a function of x (y=f(x) is the customary notation) because its value depends on the value of x. The goal of every LSS Exhibitor analysis is to find relationships (**correlations**) between variables.

In correlational analysis Exhibitors try to measure variables and look for relations between groups or sets of variables. In the Improve phase they manipulate some sets of variables and then measure the changes in effects of this manipulation on other resultants. LSS analysis typically comes down to calculating correlations between variables in order to conclusively find root causes. For example, if an Exhibitor finds that whenever they change variable A (the color of the carpet) then variable B (the number of engagements) changes, then they can conclude that "A influences B." LSS Exhibitors interpret root cause relationships based on theories or hypothesis tests for significance and they verify these causal relationships by experimenting. The tests for statistical significance are used to determine the probability that the relationships found are not purely luck or chance. If they are chance relationships they don't really have a root cause that impacts the overall show population. They only look like they do because of the way the data was sampled, measured or how they influenced the (factors) variables.

One could say that the statistical significance of a result tells something about the degree to which the result is a true representation of the population.

The first test (the null hypothesis test) determines if the differences between the groups are really important. This is done by assessing the p-value. LSS Exhibitors should understand that the higher the p-value, the less they can believe that the observed relation between variables is realistic. Specifically, the p-value represents the probability that the two groups are truly different when they really aren't. In effect it is the amount of risk being accepted by believing that the observed results are real. For example, a p-value of .05 indicates that there is a 5% chance that the relation between the variables is not realistic. In LSS models, the p-value of .05 is customarily treated as a border-line acceptable risk level because it still involves a pretty high probability of error (5%). If this number is turned around, instead of saying the Exhibitors are at risk with a 5% chance of error they say they are confident that the results are realistic by 95% (this is known as the confidence interval). The more analysis performed on a data set, the more results will meet the conventional significance level by the luck of the draw. Keep in mind that the significance depends mostly on the sample size meaning, very large samples with very small interplay between variables will be significant, whereas in small samples very large interplay cannot be considered significant. For example interviewing two Attendees Exhibitors might find a large difference in their activity and behavior. However given that they only interviewed two people they would make a huge error (many Exhibitors do this) if they project their responses onto the larger Attendee population because the sample size is so small.

When data is plotted onto a graph it forms a picture or a pattern. Conclusions are drawn about the underlying process based on the picture that emerges. For example: Suppose an Exhibitor is experimenting with the position of two different displays because they want to see if placement of the display effects how many Attendees try out the hands on demonstration of their offering. Placing the display in one location (A) the first day and a different location (B) the second day. The Exhibitor executes this experiment (which in LSS terms is an OFAT One Factor At a Time experiment), they collect the data, put it on a graph and it looks like this:

Number of Display Engagements by Location A or B

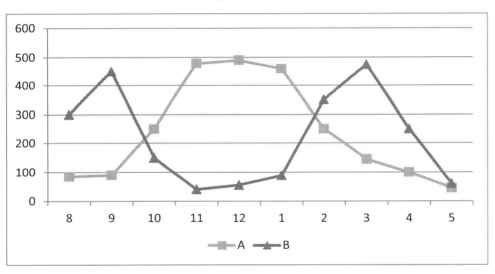

So what is the picture saying? First off notice that neither curve is "bad". It is just informative. It gives you a look into the show which allows for better decisions. Interestingly enough it is worth noting that the total (sum) of Attendees who engaged with the display on each day was almost identical. Now looking at the pictures notice that the darker graph data from location B has a (hump) peak at the 9am time and another peak at the 3pm time. This might be better for staffing the booth because some of the staff can leave at lunch and the Attendees are not left alone. A picture like this is called a bimodal curve. Bimodal curves typically indicate that what the Exhibitor thought was one process really operates as two processes and/or that something else was going on at the show that changed the traffic pattern (when doing OFATs Exhibitors take a lot of risks because of the other uncontrolled things (noises) going on around the show). But suppose the Exhibitor checks and find that the number of Attendees who passed by the booth by hour on each day was identical. Knowing that something else is going on that is influencing the Attendees to behave bimodally. This might lead the Exhibitor to watch the video and isolate behaviors. Perhaps when the display was at location B it was more visible at first and more Attendees were able to stand around it or it was easier to queue into a line to use it. The video would tell more.

The other curve starts out slow, peaks in the middle at the 12pm time and tappers off at the end. It might be that the display wasn't visible at first and once Attendees found it they crowded around to use it. This might be great in a situation where an Exhibitor is hiring staff locally because they only need them from 10-2 which would decrease their costs (5 hrs. less per staff person) for the show by more than 55%. Again watching the video would determine how this impacted the Attendees which is really the important thing. This curve is called a normal curve (sometimes a bell shaped curve because it looks like a bell). For a whole lot of reasons that are very valid but also very complex the normal curve is kind of the standard curve used for statistical testing. Most statistical test assume a normal curve distribution and this works out just fine for Orange Belt Exhibitors because the world tends to behave that way and the math is straight forward and easier.

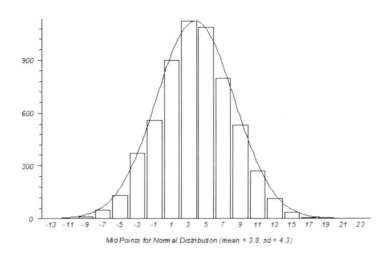

Mid Points for Normal Distribution (mean = 3.8, sd = 4.3)

Normal Curve (Normal Distribution)

Conversation about the normal curve or normal distribution typically starts by defining two things; the mean (which we already know about) because it defines where the curve is "centered" on the graph. One of the things that makes the mean easy on a normal curve is that when you look at the data half of the points in the data will be above the mean and half will be below the mean. This may seem obvious but other data curves are not like that. Suppose an Exhibitor is doing a 15 minute presentation in the booth and trying two different speakers (JP and Kelly) at two different times during the show. They measure the number of Attendees who "drop out" meaning leave the presentation after the first two minutes of presentation (they give Attendees a two minute window just in case they realize they are in the wrong presentation or the topic isn't what they thought it was). So two minutes into the presentation they start the measurement and get data which when graphed looks like this:

Graph of the number of drop outs during Presentations

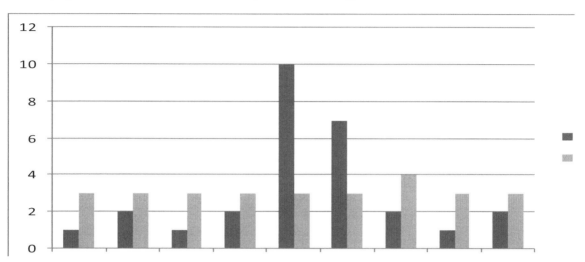

Both speakers averaged the same number of drop outs per presentation (28) but the distribution of the data reveals that JP did something different or "special" 10 minutes into the presentation that drove a lot of Attendees away. Watching the video might reveal what that activity was. If that can be fixed or changed it might result in a lower drop out rate. Kelly on the other hand has a bit more of an issue. She has a steady number of Attendees leave through out the presentation. Her problem might be more in her overall style. It is more of a common place problem for her. Fixing this might be more of a fundamental level endeavor. It might be more of a process for her. In any case the point here is that the mean tells us something but not the whole story. It is important to know where the data centers but it is also important to know how the data is spread out. How the data moves away from the center or deviates from it. This number that indicates the spread of data is called the standard deviation.

Standard Deviation

    Standard Deviation explains how much variation, spread or "dispersion" there is from the average (mean). A low standard deviation indicates that the data points tend to be very close to the mean (in the picture below the curve to the left would have a lower standard deviation than the one on the right), a high standard deviation indicates that the data points are spread out over a large range of values (the right side curve look more flattened out because it has a higher standard deviation.

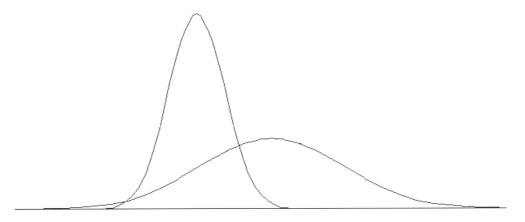

Low St.Dev. Higher St. Dev.

    One of the nice things about the standard deviation is that it can be used to break the data into segments based on how the data is dispersed from the mean. If an Exhibitor segments the curve from the mean at a point where approximately 34% of the data is on one side they will be one standard deviation away from the mean. So in a normal distribution 68% of the observed data points will fall within plus or minus one (±1) standard deviation from the mean, and a range of ±2 (sometime called 4 sigmas two on each side of the mean) standard deviations includes about 95% of the data points. By the time one gets out to ±3 (6 total) standard deviations, about

99% of the data included. If a process is working at this 6 standard deviations (or 6 sigmas) from the mean level, it is an indicator that more than 99% of the time the process is delivering a great Purchase Experience for Attendees. This is the level of a Lean Six Sigma Exhibitor, hence the name.

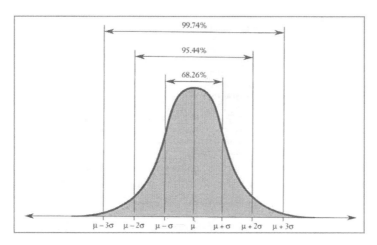

So how is knowing the shape of the normal curve useful for an LSS Exhibitor? Suppose an Exhibitor is a seller of printed books and has a Purchase Experience process where they are trying to convert Target Attendee by getting them to order a series of books by signing an order form. They time their process out and it turns out that on average it takes fifteen minutes to go through the entire process at the show. So they put cameras in their booth, record the booth during the show and time how long Attendees stay in the booth (see the graph on the following page labeled Graph 1).

What is it telling them? The curve isn't perfectly normal looking like the other graphs but that's ok. They can still do some analysis work because it looks close enough and the assumptions made won't take them too far off the track. So to start with they notice that the mean or average amount of time Attendees spend in the booth is about 14.5 minutes. At first glance that sounds ok since the process takes 15 minutes. It might be a bit too high knowing that half of the Attendees spend less than that amount of time with them but it might work. But then they look at the distribution and realize that the range which would encompass 68% of the Attendees at ±1

Graph 1

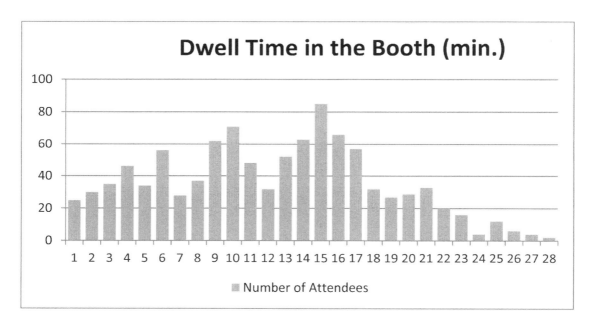

Dwell Time in the Booth (min.)

Number of Attendees

standard deviation would get down to the level of eight minutes (less than half of the time it takes to explain the process). As they go to ±2 sigma they get down to 3 minutes a fifth of what is needed and that equates to 95% of the Attendees. The conclusion they would come to after looking at the data is that the process isn't in synch with the Attendees CTQ characteristics that they value their time. To fix this they have options which they could experiment with. They could (a.) try to get Attendees to spend more time (shift the mean up and move the whole curve to the right) in the booth with them (a difficult feat since Attendees are already time constrained), or (b.)

they could find a way to shorten their process, or (c.) they could invite Attendees to a private meeting informing them that it will take about fifteen minutes. Of course there are other options but the point here is that knowing the shape of the curve allows Exhibitors to analyze the situation better and make better improvements.

Significance Tests

When looking at data LSS Exhibitors need to know if the relationship between the variables or groups is real and how strong the relationship is. To verify that there is a relationship tests for statistical significance are used and to verify the strength of the relationship, measures of association are performed. Tests for statistical significance are used to find out what the probability is that what they think is a relationship between two variables is real and not just a chance occurrence? The numbers tell what the risk level is if they assume that there is a legitimate relationship. After all one can never be 100% certain because there are too many sources of error and too many uncontrolled noise factors on the show floor.

But using probability theory and the normal curve, Exhibitors can assess the risk of assuming a relationship is true. Analysts say that the relationship is significant if the chances of being wrong are small. When differences are small but statistically significant, it is often based on a very large sample size (in a sample of a smaller size, the differences would not be enough to be statistically significant).

Steps in Testing for Statistical Significance
1. state the problem statement
2. identify the Null Hypothesis impact

3. select a level of risk (error probability (alpha level))
4. select the appropriate test for statistical significance
5. run it through the software or look it up on a table
6. analyze the results

1) State the problem statement

The problem statement identifies the relationship between two variables one might expect to see. It may be stated in general terms, but it should include dimensions of direction and magnitude.

- For example, The depth of booth training is related to the interaction rate.
- Direction: The longer the training program, the higher the interaction rate.
- Magnitude: Longer training programs will double the interaction rate.

2) Identify the Null Hypothesis impact(s)

The null hypothesis usually states that there is not a relationship between the two variables. For example, there is not a relationship between the depth of booth training and the increased interaction rate. This would be the opposite of the Exhibitor hypothesis which is that deeper booth training will lead to an increase in the interaction rate. LSS Exhibitors use the null hypothesis because it is easier to disprove the null hypothesis than it is to prove the Exhibitors' hypothesis. Meaning it is easier to show that something is false once than to show that something is true repetitively. It is easier to find non-confirming evidence that would go against the null hypothesis than to find confirming evidence for the Exhibitor hypothesis.

3) Select a level of risk (error probability (alpha level))

Even in the best LSS project, there is always a possibility (hopefully a small one) that the Exhibitor will make a mistake regarding the relationship between the two variables. There are two possible mistakes or errors.

The first is called a Type I error. This occurs when the Exhibitor assumes that a relationship exists when in fact it does not. In a Type I error, the Exhibitor accepts the null hypothesis and reject the Exhibitor hypothesis, but is wrong. The alpha is an indicator of the probability of committing a Type I error.

There is also a Type II error. This occurs when the Exhibitor believes a relationship does not exist when in fact it does. In a Type II error, the Exhibitor wrongfully rejects the null hypothesis and accepts the Exhibitor hypothesis. The beta is an indicator of the probability of committing a Type II error. The two error types are inversely related meaning reducing the chance of committing a Type I error increases the chance of committing a Type II error and vice versa.

By selecting an alpha level (inversely called a confidence level), Exhibitors select the amount of risk they are willing to take because the alpha is the probability of committing a Type I error. LSS Exhibitors typically select an alpha=.05 at most as this means they are willing to accept a probability of 5% of making a Type I error meaning they are 95% confident the relationship between the factors is legitimate. As the relationship between factors gets weaker, and/or as the level of alpha gets smaller, larger sample sizes would be used to reach statistical significance.

4) Select the appropriate test for statistical significance
Selection depends on the question being asked, the sample size and

type of data available to answer it. There is a large list of tests to choose from. Here is a sidebar review of two of them.

Sidebar - a look at a few specific tests

There are many different tests that can be done on curves to determine different characteristics. Most of them are based on the normal distribution directly or on distributions that are derived from normal distributions, such as t-test, or Chi-square which is the first test we will discuss.

Chi-Square Tests

At a <u>fundamental level </u>what the Chi Square test allows Analysts to do is take two groups of data and compare them to see if there are differences between them. This allows LSS Exhibitors to measure the booth at the show under a set of conditions (color of carpet, display location, staff process,... etc.) make changes experimentally (different carpet, different display locations, different staff process...etc.) and measure to see if the changes really did affected the Attendees. This is accomplished by plugging the numbers into a formula to obtain a Chi Statistic value (CSV). They take that CSV and assess it against a predetermined, standardized Chi Square Number from a table based on the degrees of freedom and the alpha risk level they are comfortable with. If the CSV is greater than or equal to the Chi Square Number it indicates that the changes made were significant and the affects on the Attendee are real. If it is lower than the Chi Square number it indicates that the affects were probably just coincidence or by change. Note: Chi square tests can only be used on actual numbers and not on percentages, proportions, or means. Chi-square is commonly used to compare observed data with data one would expect to obtain according to a specific hypothesis.

It is important to note that Chi Square tests for statistical significance:
- does not indicate the strength of a relationship between two variables
- does not indicate the direction of a relationship between two variables
- does not indicate the probability of a Type I error (alpha selection does)
- does not take into account the reliability and validity of the data
- does not provide absolute proof that the factor are conclusively related

When using Chi Square as a significance test:
1. state the problem statement
2. identify the Null Hypothesis impact
3. tabulate the data
4. calculate the "Chi statistic" using software (Excel, minitab, jmp...Etc.)
5. verify the degrees of freedom (df)
6. verify the level of risk (alpha level)
7. look up the actually Chi Squared value required per the df and alpha
8. interpret the results
9. move to the Improve Phase

Once a Chi statistic is obtained Exhibitors need to interpret it in context which requires two things. The first is an assessment of the degrees of freedom. The term "degrees of freedom" refers to the size of the contingency table on which the value of the CSV has been computed. The second thing needed for assessment is a selection of the level of confidence (alpha) desired. The level of alpha can vary, but the smaller the value, the more stringent the requirement for reaching statistical significance becomes.

Using the df and alpha the Chi Square Number can be looked up on a table. The Chi Squared Number is then compared to the CSV. The Chi Square, at a given level of alpha and with a given degree of freedom, is a type of "pass-fail" measurement. Either the CSV reaches the required level for statistical significance or it does not. If the value we obtain for CSV is larger than the Chi Square Number it indicates the level of statistical significance between the two variables exists. If not the relationship does not exist. However, the larger the degrees of freedom, the larger the value of CSV will need to be in order to reach statistical significance. Similarly, the higher the alpha, the larger the value of CSV will need to be to reach statistical significance.

For example;
Problem statement; In depth training of staff people increases the number of interactions in the booth.

If the computed value (CSV) is 70.42 which exceeds the Chi Square Number of 3.84 from the table for alpha (p)=.05 and df=1, then the Exhibitor can reject the null hypothesis (with only a 5% probability of error or a 95% confidence) and accept the Exhibitor hypothesis from the problem statement that a relationship exists between depth of training program attended and the increase in interaction rates. In other words one can say with 95% confidence that the deep level of training is increasing the rate of interaction between Target Attendees and exhibit staff.

As before if you want to know more on the calculation (it isn't necessary but I hope you do) look on our website www.bbmgo.com or there are plenty of amazing internet sites with video tutorials. So let's review another test.

T-tests

One of the common tests used is the **t-test**. It is used to assess the differences between two groups based on their averages or means to see how different they are from each other. If an Exhibitor has data from a show and they make changes because of an experiment they are doing at a different show they will want to know if the changes effected the Attendees. Comparing the data from the two shows would tell the impact. Looking at the graph of the data (via histograms) one could first determine if it looks normally distributed. Next they would perform a t-test to assesses whether or not the means of the two groups are statistically different from each other. This analysis is appropriate whenever someone wants to compare the means of two groups, and especially appropriate as the analysis for the post test following an experiment. (Recall the book seller example where they wanted to shift the mean so that on average Attendees would spend 15 minutes with them.)

What does it mean to say that the averages for two groups are statistically different? The average is said to be a measure of central location of the set of values or data group. Since the average is a measure of location, it only makes sense to use averages to compare two data sets or groups. Consider these three situations.

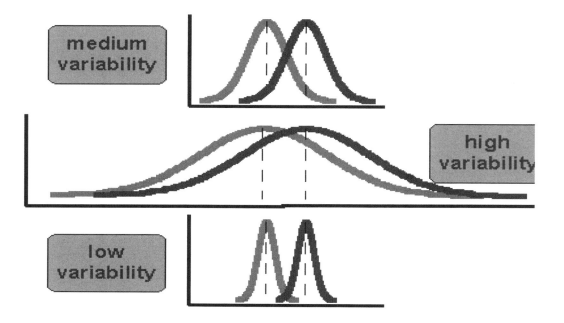

The first thing to notice about the three situations is that the difference between the means is the same in all three. But, also notice that the three situations don't look the same -- they tell very different stories. The top example shows a case with moderate standard deviation within each group. The second situation shows the high standard deviation and the third shows the case with low standard deviation. One might conclude that the two bottom low standard deviation groups appear most different because there is very little overlap between the two curves. The middle example high standard deviation group overlap so much that it appears the difference between them is negligible. The t-test allows Exhibitors to judge the difference between the means of the curves relative to the spread of the curves. It allows this because the t-test is a ratio that when reviewed with the alpha level and the degrees of freedom (df) indicates if the difference between the means for the two groups is realistic and the change has impacted (hopefully in a positive manner) the Attendees.

Note; when conducting tests of statistical significance always document:
1) the problem statement or hypothesis being considered
2) the test statistic used and its value
3) the degrees of freedom
4) the value for alpha (p-value) along with the results.

F-ratio

The F-ratio compares the data to itself and to the other data group(s) (the within and the between subgroup variation). The F-ratio is calculated by dividing specific Mean Squares by the Mean Square Error. F-ratio is related to the effect of the factor(s) and is used to determine whether the variances in two independent samples are equal. If the F-ratio is not statistically significant standard t-test for the difference of means may be used. If the F-ratio is statistically significant, use an alternative t-test computation.

Steps for F-ration analysis:
Step 1. Collect the summary statistics.
For example;
Sample A S^2=20 n=10   *(S^2 is the variance)*
Sample B S^2=30 n=30

Step 2. Determine the degrees of freedom (df) for each sample
df = n1 - 1 (numerator = n for sample with larger variance)
df for numerator (Sample B) = 29
df = n2 - 1 (denominator = n for sample with smaller variance)
df for denominator (Sample A) = 9

Step 3. Determine the level of confidence -- alpha
Consult F-Distribution table for df = (29,9), alpha.05
f critical value (Fcv)= 2.70

Step 4. Compute the Test Statistic by dividing the largest variance (S^2) by the smallest (F = 30/20 = 1.5)

Step 5. Compare the test statistic (1.5) with the f critical value (2.70) Since the test statistic (1.50) did not meet or exceed the critical value (2.70) there is no statistically significant difference between the variance exhibited in Sample A and the variance exhibited in Sample B. Consequently other factors should be manipulated and experimented with until a significant positive effect is achieved. A "failed experiment" is a learning opportunity.

Correlations Analysis

Correlation is a measure of the relationship between two or more variables. Correlation coefficients (r) range from -1.00 to +1.00 which determines the extent to which values of the two variables are "proportional" to each other. (The value of -1.00 represents a perfect negative correlation which means the two variable are opposite of each other while a value of +1.00 represents a perfect positive correlation meaning they work perfectly in synch. A value of 0.00 represents a complete lack of correlation). Proportional means the correlation can be graphed along a straight line (sloped upwards or downwards). This straight line is called the regression line or least squares line. In order to evaluate the correlation between variables, it is important to know the "magnitude" or "strength" (r squared) as well as the significance of the correlation. Both will change depending on the size of the sample from which it was computed.

ANOG (Analysis of Good)

Another analysis technique is ANOG or Analysis of Good. ANOG is a practical method used to identify patterns in the type of response data you get when doing experiments. To perform ANOG, simply order the data results from best results to worst results. Then analyze each column to see if any column has a distinguishable pattern or trend.

Normal plots

Normal plots help pick out effects that are not on a straight line and typically not expected results. Unexpected usually occur because factor at one level are from a different population or are changing from one level to another which changes the result (a significant event). Typically the farther a point deviates from the straight line or regression line, the more likely it is significant.

To create a normal plot:
1. arrange effects in ascending order
2. choose appropriate normal plot graph
3. select a scale on the horizontal axis
4. plot the data on the graph. The smallest value is plotted on line 1 (short). The second point is plotted on line 2. I repeat this for all the data points.
5. label data points with factor effects
6. analyze - draw a straight line of best fit through the data
7. calculate the line that fits the data
8. calculate how far data points are from the line(-1 to 0 to 1) scale coefficient tells you the variability of the data

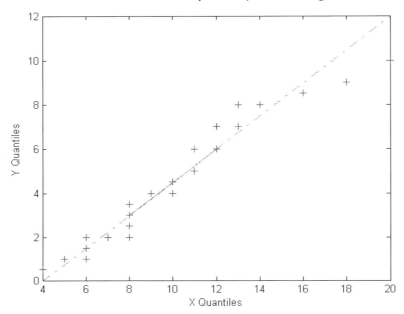

Normal Probability Plot (with a regression line)

COV (Components of Variation)

Components of Variation (COV) is a tool set that identifies the factors that are causing variation and impacting the Attendees. Through use of Chi Squared, COV looks at what changes within subgroup and between sub-groups as well as what is in control and out of control for the different levels of the process structure. Most software will do COV analysis at the click of a mouse but here is the process for doing COV analysis.

1. Put it into a table
2. graph it (scatter plot)
3. regress the data
4. put data into a quartile
5. Analyze the Chi-Squared

COV helps to identify if there is a need to take continuous measure-ments of the stability of the system being studied. This will determine how many groups to sample, what type of study to do (crossed or nested) and if it is even worth while to do the study.

Control Charts

As stated in the previous chapter Control charts are used as a means to monitor process variables (x's) and parameters (Y's). LSS Exhibitors use con-trol charts to understand the stability and variation in critical x's identified using designed experiments (DOE's) which we will learn more about in the Improve phase because they differentiate the variation. A data set that is in control is typically stable, predictable and the variation is mainly due com-mon causes. A data set that is out of control is typically unstable, unpredict-able and the variation is due to special and common causes.

When looking at control charts one can study the process to identify sources of variation and then act to eliminate or reduce those sources of variation locally. An Exhibitor can also see the extent of variation that exists so that they don't overreact to random variation If looking deep into the process by charting it at different steps and levels, Exhibitors can find the root problems and fix them.

Once the data is plotted with the upper and lower control limits Exhibi-tors might see a data point go out of the limits. This is an indicator of a special cause event. Instead of spending time fixing the process time spent looking into what happened that was unique or assignable to some unique activity is required. Using the FMEA an Exhibitor should then evaluate the RPN of the event and take appropriate precautions to diminish the risk.

X - R CONTROL CHART SAMPLE

Order Processing Times

X Chart	R Chart
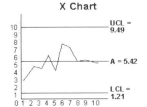	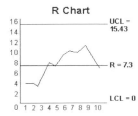

Here are other situtations to watch for when using control charts;

- seeing 6 or 8 points above the centerline which then switch below the center line can indicate a cause, if the range of the chart is in control.
- A point beyond the control limits (out of control limits)
- Six points in a row steadily increasing or decreasing.
- Fourteen points in a row alternating up and down (saw-tooth pattern).
- Two out of three points in a row outside the control limits.
- Fifteen points in a row below the centerline. "hugging the centerline" or "white space" implies stratification within the subgroups
- Eight points in a row on both sides of the centerline

Just because data is in control doesn't mean that the process is good and it doesn't mean that the Purchase Experience is satisfactory or without problems. Control charts can identify problems but they don't solve problems. They gives clues as to what is going on. The exhibit team solves the problems that the control charts indicate.

LSS Exhibitors need to experience the event over the time of the sampling to understand the control chart data. If it is a common event (the factor effects are bad every day) then a day or so of data is enough to locate the problem. If they only get bad groups occasionally or so then they need to sample for a few events. Try to collect data in ways that it answers more than one question. If a chart that is in control it just means that the source of variation is common or noise. If it is out of control that means that there are special causes in effect.

ANOVA (Analysis of Variation)

As a study becomes increasingly complicated, more complex statistical measures must also be used which is where ANOVA comes in to play. Similar to t-tests, Analysis of variance (ANOVA) is a statistical method used for comparing sample means to identify if they are truly different. However, t-tests compare only two sample distributions and ANOVA is capable of comparing many.

Suppose an Exhibitor is conducting a study on Attendee opinions regarding the product or service offering, and rated a sample of 100 Attendees on a scale of 1 to 10 (1 = passed-by only, 10 = interacted face to face) based on the quality of their consumption in the booth (Purchase Experience Rating or PER). The main objective for the study is to determine if there is a difference in the PER, depending on the Attendees Buying potential. As such, the independent variable or factor would be BUYING LEVEL (BL), consisting of 4 levels: 1. No currently a buyer, 2. Recommender, 3. Occasional buyer, 4. Main Buyer. The dependent variable would be Purchase Experience provided in the booth (PER). In theory, one could do multiple t-tests instead of a single ANOVA but ANOVA offers numerous advantages that t-tests can not provide. Specifically, ANOVA allows the Exhibitor to avoid over inflated alpha effects that arise from using multiple t-tests. When running a t-test an alpha or p-value less than .05 because a p<.05 means the probability of getting statistically significant results simply by chance is less than 5%. However multiple t-tests lead to erroneous rejection of the Exhibitor hypothesis. In this example, the hypothesis is that no significant differences exist in booth rating by buyer type. Rejection of the Exhibitor hypothesis is also known as a Type 1 error or a false positive.

The more t-test conducted the higher the probability of getting a Type 1 error. In the example, there are only six possible t-tests so alpha inflation is not as big of a problem as it might be in a bigger test. Suppose the Exhibitor was testing the effectiveness of ten different types of displays. The number of t-test comparisons that can be done in this sample would be 45! See below:

Display 1 vs. Display 2, Display 2 vs. Display 9 Display 5 vs. Display 6
Display 1 vs. Display 3, Display 2 vs. Display 10, Display 5 vs. Display 7
Display 1 vs. Display 4, Display 3 vs. Display 4, Display 5 vs. Display 8
Display 1 vs. Display 5, Display 3 vs. Display 5, Display 5 vs. Display 9
Display 1 vs. Display 6, Display 3 vs. Display 6, Display 5 vs. Display 10
Display 1 vs. Display 7, Display 3 vs. Display 7, Display 6 vs. Display 7
Display 1 vs. Display 8, Display 3 vs. Display 8, Display 6 vs. Display 8
Display 1 vs. Display 9, Display 3 vs. Display 9, Display 6 vs. Display 9
Display 1 vs. Display 10, Display 3 vs. Display 10, Display 6 vs. Display 10
Display 2 vs. Display 3, Display 4 vs. Display 5, Display 7 vs. Display 8
Display 2 vs. Display 4, Display 4 vs. Display 6, Display 7 vs. Display 9
Display 2 vs. Display 5, Display 4 vs. Display 7, Display 7 vs. Display 10

Display 2 vs. Display 6, Display 4 vs. Display 8, Display 8 vs. Drug 9
Display 2 vs. Display 7, Display 4 vs. Display 9, Display 8 vs. Display 10
Display 2 vs. Display 8, Display 4 vs. Display 10, Display 9 vs. Display 10

In addition to opening the door for alpha inflation this would be cumbersome and time consuming. One is better off running the ANOVA, to determine if any differences exist in the first place, and then running specific t-tests to determine where those differences lie. Returning to the example a spreadsheet for this study on PER of the booth might look like this:

Buyer Level	PER Rating
1	10
1	5
2	8
2	3
3	5
3	9
4	7
4	9

A one-way ANOVA can be conducted on this data, with PER as the dependent measure, and BL (with four levels) as the independent measure. The mean PER for each BL are shown in the output and figure on the following page:

BL	N	Mean PER	St. Dev.	SE	Min	Max
1	20	8.35	1.53	.34	6	10
2	24	7.75	2.13	.44	4	10
3	45	8.04	2.26	.34	2	10
4	11	6.27	3.32	1.0	2	10
Total	100	7.84				

When running the data one ends up with a set of data that looks like the next table, don't be surprised at the unbalanced appearance.

Groups	Sum of Squares	df	Mean Squares	F	p
Between Groups	34.297	3	11.432	2.272	.085
Within Groups	483.143	96	5.033		
Total	517.440	99			

The F-score and p-value of a one-way ANOVA will indicate whether the main effect of the independent variable "Buyer Level" was significant. In other words, the F-statistic would tell us that Buyer Level had a significant effect on PER. In this example, the p-value of .085 suggests that a marginally significant difference exists within comparisons of PER among the four buyer levels. Although the ANOVA results tell that BL related differences exist in PER, it does not tell where the differences lie. Is it between BL 1 and 4, 1 and 2, 3 and 4. To find that Exhibitors need to look at the rest of the post-hoc test results (a series of t-tests). The results of the post-hoc tests as follows:

BL (A)	vs. BL (B)	Mean (A to B)	SE	p-value
1	2	.60	.679	.379
1	3	.31	.603	.613
1	4	2.08*	.842	.015
2	3	-.29	.567	.605
2	4	1.48	.817	.074
3	4	1.77*	.755	.021

BUYING LEVEL (BL): 1. No currently a buyer, 2. Recommender, 3. Occasional buyer, 4. Main Buyer.

So what does this indicate? Two groups have means significantly (p<.05) different from each other. 4's (Main Buyers) seem to have a significantly higher rating than both 1's and 3's (p=.015 and .021 respectively). 4's also rate a little bit higher than 2's (p=.074). What this shows is that "Main Buyers" seem to consume the booth space Purchase Experience more than any other level including "occasional buyers". Attendees who need the product often and purchase it often spend more time at the booth, engage with more displays, pick up more literature and interact with staff for a longer period of time than other categories.

Why did the overall ANOVA show only a marginally significant difference (p=.085), while the pair-wise comparisons yielded two differences (i.e., 1's vs. 4's and 3's vs. 4's) that were strongly significant? This is because the overall ANOVA compares all values simultaneously, thus weakening statistical power. The post-hoc tests are simply a series of independent t-tests.

The ultimate goal of analysis tools is to create a model. This is accomplished by defining an equation that represents the relationship between the factors and the resultant. This is often in the mathematical form of $Y=f(x)$. In it's simplist form "transfer equations" will reveal the main effects as well as the interplay effects. For example if an experiment was run in the booth changing the color of the carpeting (x_1), while simultaneously using different displays (x_2) and either having a staff person present or not present(x_3) the following transfer equation would be generated with the spaces filled by coefficients and/or exponents and the $\mathscr{E}$ representing the error term;

$$Y = \_x_1^{..} + \_x_2^{..} + \_x_3^{..} + \_x_{12}^{..} + \_x_{13}^{..} + \_x_{23}^{..} + \_x_{123}^{..} + \mathscr{E}$$

$$\underbrace{\qquad\qquad}_{\text{main effects}} \quad \underbrace{\qquad\qquad}_{\text{2-way interplays}} \quad \underbrace{\quad}_{\text{3-way}}$$

This equation would be used to model the causal relationships between the factors andn the resultant which in this example would be the number of Target Attendees attracted into the booth space. Designed experiments like this which will be explained in more detail in the next chapter, are used to create these models.

The Analyze phase tools reveal the root causes of defects and errors. Knowing what is causing the issues takes the guess work out of solving problems. Once the causes are identified the Improve phase tools are used to create solutions and experiments to verify the depth and breadth of the fix and the effect on the Target Attendees and/or Customers.

Define 〉〉 Implement 〉〉 Measure 〉〉 Analyze 〉〉 Improve 〉〉 Control

Chapter 6

Improve Phase

Right the Ship

When LSS Exhibitors are talking about improvements they are typically talking about either;

- reducing the range or variation in the process
- shifting the mean of the process
- or both

They do this by using the data analysis from the previous phase to identify root causes, factors (x's) and noises that are truly affecting the Target Attendees in the Purchase Experience process. Armed with the knowledge of the process and the causes of variation they set up experiments in the Improve phase and inject them back into the DIMAIC process as the show cycle repeats. Prior to formulating experiments they figure out why they are experimenting with specific variables and they communicate this to all team members. Focusing on the resultant Y's they decide what X's (factors and noises) to look at and change. LSS Exhibitors change the process to get it within the specifications that suite the Target Attendees first then move the overall process (mean shift) to get it centered around the specification. They do this by looking at common causes and noises and not just special causes. This requires the Exhibitor team to think outside the box and not just experiment on factors that they don't think they can change or that they have tried to change before unsuccessfully. With this in mind it is a good idea to start the Improve phase off with a good brainstorming session.

Brainstorming

In the define phase some suggestions on how to conduct a good brainstorming session were given. It is good practical technique for analysis and problem solving. Here are some different methods to consider in executing a brainstorming session. The first is to go around the room and everyone gets a turn to express an idea. The second is to allow everyone to randomly call out ideas and the third is to have everyone put ideas down on index cards which are collected, categorized and sorted for similarities. Make sure managers are dispersed among workers so that the social political capital is reduced. Capture every idea for how to improve the process. Don't allow anyone to feel intimidated or devalued

Cover the following when brainstorming for improvements:
- What is working versus what is not working. Why?
- Are there solutions that have been tried unsuccessfully? What made them fail? Have conditions changed that might allow success?
- If we could wave a magic wand and change this, what would we change?
- Are the ideas and potential solutions feasible?
- Have these solutions been tried before?
- Compare the as-is state to the to-be state on the migration plan.
- Consider noise factors or other uncontrolled parameters in your processes and projects that might drift over time and invalidate the results of your process work and experimentation.
- Develop strategies for understanding whether such factors do impact the work. Expect to see alternate strategies and strengths and weaknesses of each strategy.
- Upon discovery develop strategies for dealing with these factors in the processes.
- What collaborators could provide solutions?
- Discuss how you will know whether the experimental results are repeatable and sustainable.

Value Stream Mapping (VSM)

In the Analyze phase value stream maps were created. Value stream mapping has become essential for many organizations and there are a vast number of resources and examples of them on the internet. There is also a vast number of standardized icons which are used for the different activities and process steps involved in business applications. Most LSS Exhibitor teams can typically get by with the squares, ovals and diamonds (decisions are typically in diamonds) and they also find it useful to first create a "Current State Map" which reflects how the process is currently performing. All the measurements, flows, and steps should reflect how things are running as of today. Once LSS Exhibitors have the current state mapped out their focus turns to areas for improvement. Activities such as root cause analysis and brainstorming are done to see how the waste in these areas can be eliminated or reduced. With these improvements identified they create a new map called the "Future State Map". This is the continuation of the example from the previous chapter with the changes to reflect the future state.

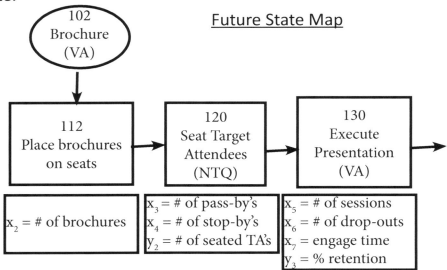

The Future State Map captures the changes and actions which are then implemented into the business processes permanently and/or as experiments.

Decision Mapping

During the Implement phase decision maps were introduced as a means to depict how a decision process works. During the Improve phase these maps are now used to evaluate the effects to the decision process based on changes made to the Purchase Experience by the Exhibitor. For example if the Exhibitor executes an experiment focused on attracting more TA's into the booth it would be nice to know what the initial state is, implement the experiment and then measure to see if things changed. The decision map is used to graphically display the before and after in order to assess the probability of the Purchase Experience moving one direction or another relative to the ROI (return on investment).

For example suppose that an Exhibitor spends approximately $850,000 at an event and draws 40% of the Attendees off the aisle into face to face interactions (850) with the booth staff. During the 850 Target Attendee (TA) interactions the staff performs a conversion closing process which consists of an agreed upon appointment within a 30 day period following the show. The Exhibitor follows up post show and converts approximately 10% of the meetings into closed sales averaging $17,000 per sale.

The decision mapping would now include the percentages or probabilities of the activities and smaller dashed lines to show the locations where no information is exchanged.

Here is what the decision map would look like at this point. Notice that there are lines of restriction at two points where the TA does not enter the booth and where the TA does not interact. These restriction points exist because there is no contact between the Exhibitor (2) and the TA (1) at these points and subsequently no information is exchanged. In order to overcome the restriction the Exhibitor would have to find a way to make sure every Target Attendee entered the booth and interacted. This would be an entirely different project focus for experimentation.

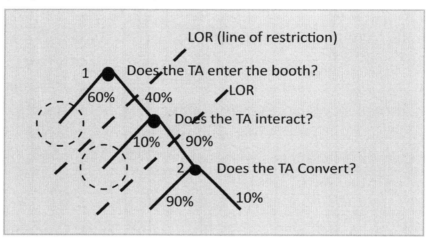

Utilizing the decision map data the revenue for the show can now be assessed by taking 85 closing sales (10% of the 850 appointments) and multiplying it against the sales value of $17,000 which yields total revenue of $1,445,000. Dividing the total costs of the show by the revenue (850,000/1,445,000=.59) reveals that the ROI is 59%.

This hefty return certainly justifies the investment and costs associated with the show and the decision map can now be evaluated as ROI improvement changes are made to the booth. Changes in the form of structured experiments.

Experimenting

One of the main strengths of Leans Six Sigma is that the process changes the way Exhibitors look at shows and events. Instead of being a place where they show up and wait for leads, shows become laboratories that allow them to gain insight into the Purchase Experience process. LSS Exhibitors often comment that in their old world they stressed about getting the booth together. Once the show was open they stressed about all the things that went wrong and all the fires they spent their days putting out. After the show they stressed about the tear down and they stressed about having to justify their budgets to management. This all changes for them once they implement Lean Six Sigma.

In the LSS world they look at every show (from setup to reporting) as another chance to manipulate factors in an experiment. They see the entire process as one great big laboratory that they can run experiments on and grow their learnings exponentially. They measure the things that are important and when things go wrong they not only understand why based on the measurements and analysis they have captured, but they see it as a failed experiment which increases their inference or learning space. While other Exhibitors live in fear of failure, LSS Exhibitors thrive on it because failures are only planned learning opportunities that get them giant steps closer to optimization.

Experiment types;
- Trial and error
- One factor at a time (OFAT)
- Full factorial
- Fractional factorial

Trial and error

This is one of the most common experiment methods and also one of the least useful. When an exhibit group uses trial and error experiments they might stumble upon a solution but they will be unable to discover why a solution worked. Since they don't know why the solution worked they can not apply the solution or knowledge about the fix to other problems. They have A SOLUTION to A PROBLEM only. It may not even be the best solution and it may not repeat or replicate. One good thing about trial and error methods is that very little knowledge is required to execute these experiments. Sometimes this works if the group has no previous knowledge and is just getting started. The issue becomes that there is very little information available after the experiment other than A SOLUTION to A PROBLEM. If trial by error experiments are repeated it might be possible to eventually find all the solutions and then determine which one is the best one but this is a very tedious, risky and expensive process. For these reasons trial and error should be viewed as a last resort for a problem resolution.

One Factor at a Time (OFAT)

OFAT experiments are the next most familiar experiment method. The premise of an OFAT is that it is possible to hold everything constant and vary only one factor at a time. While this method is a bit more sophisticated than trial and error it still doesn't provide much information or understanding about best solutions. The solution is again A SOLUTION to A PROBLEM which can only be instituted if EVERYTHING stays the same. Typically the big issue with OFATs is that the experimenter might think things are being "held constant" but they really are varying without control or monitoring. This will leave the experimenter wondering if the changes in the response variable are really due to the changed factor. In addition it is often difficult and time consuming to just change one factor at a time and try different factors at different levels. OFATs tell us what happen when one factor is changed at a time and doesn't provide any information about the relationship between the factor and other factors. OFATs therefore, have a limited inference space. Similar to trial and error the inference space only allows knowledge inside the space of the experiment meaning one can only hypothesize out-side of the space. Also more data is needed to indicate interrelations. Both of these experiment types limit the ability of the experimenter to hone in on the factors and levels that truly impact the Target Attendee.

Full Factorials

The next two types of experiments reflect a more structured design and are typically grouped under the term DOE's or Design of Experiments. They come in many formats but the most common type are "full factorials and fractional factorials" They both allow for a massive and powerful increase in knowledge about factors and their impact on Target Attendees in the Purchase Experience. They assist in the identification of what factors impact Target Attendees but that is only part of the story. Understanding the size or level of the factor and the way a factor relates to other factors in driving At-tendee behavior is the key to success and DOE's deliver that understanding.

With full factorials it is possible to examine every possible combination of factors at different levels which enables Exhibitors to not only determine the "main effects" of the factors but also the interplay or combination effects of multiple factors. These interplays between factors and selected response variables are grouped as "2-ways, 3-ways, 4-ways...etc." depend-ing on how many factors are manipulated. As a result the inference space is larger than with Trial/Error or OFAT methods with no loss of statistical validity. Exhibitors get more useful data about the factors and they need less experiment repetitions and runs meaning they can learn more with fewer "treatments" or shows.

Full factorials are often mapped out in arrays (like the one on the next page). Designing an experiment starts with the selection of factors that are of interest based on learnings accrued in the Analysis phase. These factors are then manipulated at levels in order to test the effect of the factors at a range (high and low) of points. For example; Exhibitor booths can prevent Attendees from freely entering using design and behavior factors in combination. The color of the booth carpet when strongly divergent from the color of the aisle carpet will create a forcefield effect. If the booth properties are build as high walls around the perimeter of the booth it will create a castlewall effect which also prevents free flow into the space. Finally the staff members standing along the wall will create a sentry duty effect which further inhibits entry. Each of these factors by itself is an inhibitor but when an Exhibitor combines them the three way combination has a substantially larger repulsion effect than the main effects of any one factor. Before going any further here is some DOE terminology.

Factors elements of the experiment that will typically be varied at a high and low level or high, medium and low level. These are the things that influence TA's (x's, noises,...etc.). When the factors are elements an Exhibitor can change or manipulate they are denoted as x's. When they are not elements that can be manipulated they are referred to as noises. DOE's have multiple factors and these factors are set at different levels. There are a variety of strategies used to deal with noises such as blocking.

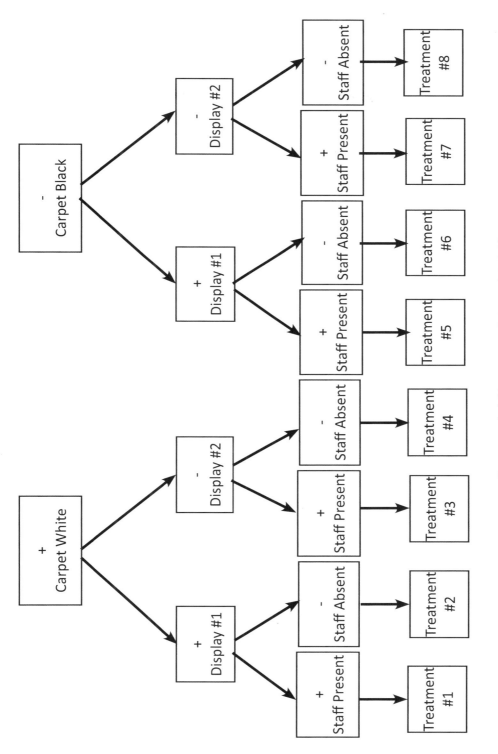

Full Factorial (3 Factor, 2 Level DOE)

Level The values of the factors in the DOE. Typically this is a high and a low for a 2 level design or a high, medium and low for a 3 level design. It is vital that levels are never set beyond what would realistically be implemented. For Example, samples might be a factor in an experiment and there is no doubt that a lifetime supply of the offering would attract 100% of the Attendees into the booth. However, a factor set at this high level would be unrealistic due to the obvious fact that no Exhibitor could ever be profitable with this high, unrealistic level. Never test factors at level that are unrealistic! Ever!! Setting the levels for factor is critical. If levels are too close together, not enough variation will be available to analyze (measurement system may not be discriminate enough). Confounding may occur and it will be impossible to separate the results for each level. If the levels are too far apart, unrealistic variation may be created which biases the analysis. Non-linear relationships may go undetected and conclusions about the broad inference space will be erroneous. The more levels a factor is tested at, the more knowledge can be gained about the impact on TA's.

Combination An item of the experiment that defines the interplay between factors of a particular level with each other (sometimes referred to as "2-way interplays when there are 2 factors involved and 3-way interplays with 3 factors...etc.. For example, an experiment with 2 factors (A & B) each with 2 levels (A-high, A-low, B-high,B-low) would have 4 possible interplay combinations: A-high to B-high, A-low to B-high, A-high to B-low, A-low to B-low)

Inference Space The area within which someone draws conclusions based on the results of the experiment. This is critical in determining; how to run the experiment, how much data is needed, when the data should be collected, and in what order the data should be collected. Adding factors makes the space broader. Increased distance between levels also increases the inference space. When thinking about experiments it is helpful to think about going hiking on a mountain. If a person decided to go hiking how do you know what equipment to bring and how to dress? The answer is they don't know unless given some information about the size of the mountain, the steepness of the mountain, how high they are going to climb, the climate of the mountain range, its' location and proximity to resources. In short there is a myriad of things they need to know. They need information in order to infer what equipment is needed. The amount of information determines the inference space. More information means a larger inference space.

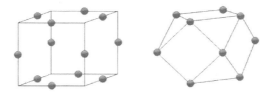

(different DOE designs create different mathematical inference spaces)

Block Sometimes factors, noises...etc. are lumped together in an experiment or set as experimental boundaries. This is common in DOE's that have elements that can not be easily manipulated. These items are referred to as blocks and the use of them is called blocking. The block is treated as a factor. However, if the block turns out to be impactful more experiments should be run separating out the factors in the block if possible.

When designing experiments always consider:
- How factors and levels are allocate to the experiment and the potential interplay between factors and levels
- What assumptions are made in the analysis of the resulting design.

- Most often there is a strong relationship between the allocation component and the analysis component of experimental design. Be aware that the experiment factors are precious and time at a show is in limited supply.

Fractional Factorial Experiments

It often makes the most sense to do a DOE with a small number of factors (never more than 5) in order to simplify the analysis and minimize the costs. Sometimes the manipulation of the factors and execution of the DOE might not be expensive, but each combination might be difficult to achieve. In shows with union contractors the charges to move displays around might be prohibitive to execution of a seemingly simple DOE. Getting staff people stay off their phones or avoid clustering together are difficult especially as the show slows down. Doing more smaller experiments is more effective than fewer large experiments. So it is important to minimize the number of combinations tried when possible.

A common DOE is one with all factors set at two levels each. These levels (high and low) are often noted on a chart as `+1' and `-1', respectively. As previously stated a design with all possible high/low combinations run is called a full factorial design. Sometimes it is not feasible or necessary due to constraints to execute every combination run of the experiment. When this avails itself the DOE can be executed by only running certain factor combinations. In cases like this where the full factorial is not completely run the DOE is said to be fractionated and is called a "fractional factorial". LSS Exhibitors will often do fractional factorials to screen out certain factors and then do full factorials when levels and factors have been finalized in order to zero in on the exact levels and interplay effects. As the knowledge base increases the level of detail the Exhibitor needs increases. This is akin to the idea that when going from Chicago to Boston a traveler doesn't need a detailed map of Boston. They need a higher level map (fractional factorial) of the upper United States. However once they get to Boston the detail street map (full factorial) becomes vital.

It is extremely important to consider how data from a DOE is analyzed. The data that is collected needs to be consistent with the proposed analysis. If, for example, the LSS Exhibitor collects only fractional factorial data, then only a fractional-factorial analysis can be completed. Because they are manipulating multiple factors at multiple levels techniques from the Analysis phase like ANOVA and Control Charting become the optimal tools for identifying the variation within and between factors as well as in and out of control processes.

Here are some points to live by when doing DOE's;
- Don't be afraid to be wrong - much is learned by a "failed experiment"
- Document everything - be punctilious
- Keep a journal of failed experiments
- Don't be afraid to deal with constructive/tribal knowledge-ideas
- Don't be afraid of theory(s)-Test them
- Manipulate variables if and when possible
- Know what to look for
- Let the questions lead
- Identify what factors will change and what will be kept the same
- The purpose of initial tests is not to solve the problem. The purpose is to determine where we need to work to solve the problem.
- Start small and grow through your successes and failures

Q-Map for Experiments

Same as before all phases including the Improve phase start with question map updating. This becomes particularly important when designing experiments. Questions to ask when setting up any experiment:

- How many runs can be made?
- Are noise variables an issue or concern?
- Are interplays suspected?
- Are some factors harder to change than others?
- How can the experiment be replicated?
- How can the experiment be repeated?
- How should the experiment be run?
- What is the goal of the experiment (optimization, screening, regression, prediction)?
- Is the response qualitative or quantitative?
- Is the response variable nominal is best, larger is better, smaller is better or dynamic in nature?
- Is the concern for process centering, process variation, or both?
- What is the process baseline (e.g. average and sigma) for the response variable?
- Where are we today?
- What x's and noises are changing over the comparison time?
- Is the response variable currently in statistical control?
- Is the response variable affected by time?
- How much of a change in response variable detection is desired?
- Do you know the expected distribution of the response variable?
- Is the measurement system adequate?
- Are there multiple responses to be concerned with?
- What are the priorities for optimization?

- What is the problem?
- When does it need to be done?
- What is the history of the problem (new/old)?
- Has something been changed recently and then this problem occurred?
- Or has it always been there to varying degree?
- What data type is being looked at (attribute/variable)?
- What is the current level of variation?
- Why is it bad?
- How is bad/good determined?
- Is the variation run to run, show to show, (same show and booth)?
- What is the Y? (outputs)?
- Are there other Y's in the system that can be affected if the Exhibitor messes with this Y?
- How are we going to measure the Y's?
- Is the measurement system repeatable and reliable?
- What is the error in the measurement system?
- What are the parts of the system contributing to the error?
- Can you separate the measurement error and the show variation?
- When variation is run to run with a show, how much of the variation is due to measurement system and how much is due to the actual show variation?
- What is the sampling subgroups/timing that should be used?
- What is the physics of the process?
- What is the process map?
- What is the Target Attendee specification?
- Are we measuring the right things the right way?
- What are the x's in the process?
- Do we need to measure them?

- Can we measure them?
- How are we going to measure them?
- Do we need to monitor the noise?
- What is the FMEA?
- What is the history?
- What is the desired resolution?
- How are we going to monitor them?
- What effects do you want to estimate?
- How are we going to measure them?
- How many samples do I need?
- How many runs should I make?
- How can I be confident in my results?
- Should we run a big DOE or a bunch of smaller ones?
- How can we tell if we are setting the levels correctly?

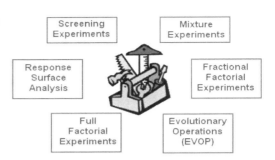

Factor Relationship Diagrams (FRD)

Factor Relationship Diagrams or FRD's are tools that are used to graphically display an experiment. These are sometimes considered Experimentation Plans as it absolutely MUST be done before any experiment in order to clearly understand what and where the restrictions of the experiment are. This tool allows the Exhibitor to understand what background variables are aligning with the factors. It also allows for the ability to visualize the structure and set the factors and levels which is critical. Exhibitors must be careful that the setup of the experiment isn't aligning with the factors. Resetting the booth is important especially when running confirmation runs. This affects whether it is a repeat or a replication of the DOE.

FRD is a planning tool used to make sure that the information obtained is the information desired. It is a good idea to lay out 3 or 4 different FRDs for the same DOE and then figure out which is really providing the desired information. This helps the LSS Exhibitor understand where they need to randomize and where they need to block. That way they can be certain that the noise aligns in an area that doesn't affect the results they are looking for.

A typical simplified FRD example:

```
booth          -      +
setup          1      2
block          1      2
------------------------------------- line of restriction
DOE design matrix goes down here
```

It is so important to do detailed FRD's because it helps Exhibitors avoid mistakes. FRD's for fractional factorial should be done by first making the structure of the full factorial. Then tracing out the legs used for the fractional factorial. Making sure the DOE structure and the parts of the structure relating to the COV and MSE are included. Indicate what things are blocked with the factors.

Look at the degree of freedom above the line of restriction. If there are 8 runs above the line, there are 7 degrees of freedom. If there are 2 samples taken from the booth at different times over a 3 day show, there are 6 runs. 8 df have already used (7 df + 1 df to estimate the mean). Thus there are 7 left over. The factors above the line of resolution are written in 1 color and indicated with + and - signs. The factors below the line of resolution are written in another color and listed as numbers 1,2,3.....n. It is important to understand what the Exhibitor is trying to accomplish with the testing. This will help clarify how to set up the tree structure which can then be adjusted so the results can be analyzed.

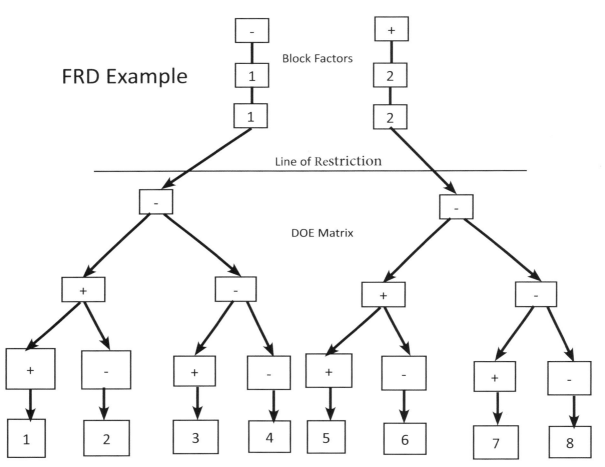

(FRD with an arrayed DOE Matrix with three factors at two levels which creates eight treatment combinations. The experimental array is below a line of restriction created by factors that are blocked together. These blocked factors could be day of show, time of day or other noises that are a part of the show. Blocked factors can be pulled out if they become significant to the experiment.)

Poka Yoke (Mistake Proofing)

A Japanese phrase which basically means mistake proofing, Poka Yoke can be used to tune process steps and also for designing a new system altogether. During the Improve phase, the possibilities for eliminating a major cause of errors can be explored by improving or redesigning the system to avoid error-inducing scenarios.

Mistake proofing is about adding controls to prevent defects, reduce their severity, and detect them if they occur. Poka Yoke is often used as a corrective action tool. FMEA can help identify the modes of the defects and failures but Poka Yoke helps implement actions to correct it. There are various levels, effort, and costs of error proofing which the team should identify prior to implementation.

There are three types of Poka Yokes:
•Contact method - identifies defects through testing characteristics.
•Fixed-value - a specific number of repeated corrective activities.
•Sequence method - structured SOP activity.

An example of Poka Yoke in action: A large number of hands on demonstrations were being cancelled abruptly. Demonstration units gave Attendees a standard set of action buttons for each step of the demonstration: "Approve to Next" and "Approve to Close." The former approved the step and sent the demonstration forward, while the latter approved the step but ended the demonstration. The FMEA showed that the cause for the high number of terminations was the confusing nomenclature on the buttons. The issue was resolved (using Poka Yoke), by eliminating the close button and providing an "exit" button on the upper corner of the screen.

Ultimately if the booth space is defective it can affect the Attendee in intangible ways and ruin the reputation of the Exhibitor which can lead to large tangible cost. Ultimately this may raise objections that can not be overcome during conversion. Each step of the process should be error-proofed to ensure defects are not passed on to the next step. For example, a faulty or defective displays will not be efficient in driving the Attendee through the conversion process. They may also send a signal that the Exhibitor produces faulty unsafe products which would have to be overcome later.

While working with a company called R2 Technology the LSS team discovered (VOC) that Target Attendees did not feel their two main software products integrated well with other (the #1 objection to purchasing the software). An FMEA revealed that there was a failure mode in getting Target Attendees to see both products working together which was brought on by the booth design. TA's were taken to one side of the booth to see one software and another side of the booth to see the other. Poka Yoke was used to integrate both software programs onto all the demo units. Interestingly enough seeing the two products together overcame the objection and R2 tripled their annual sales at the RSNA Annual Meeting.

Other examples of Poka Yoke
Spell check on word editors
UPC codes and scanners
Circuit breaker on displays
Booth staff training
Low fuel alarm and visual indicator on cars
Automatic save features on software
Pull down menus
The hole in the upper portion of a sink to prevent overflow

Pressure relief valve on hot water heater
Coffee maker shut off feature when pot is removed
Tinting of contact lenses to assist in locating them
L or R on the contact lens case to indicate left eye and right eye
Kill switch of jet-ski attached to life jacket
Product labels, keyboard labels, cash register labels
On lights for materials, maintenance, or assistance
"Are you sure you want to DELETE" reminder on software programs
Sorting of suspect material

The solutions developed during the Improve phase are plugged back into the DIMAIC process for implementation at the show as the cycle repeats. Once permanent solutions are found they are institutionalized using the Control phase tools.

Chapter 7

Control Phase

Set Sail for the Revolution

This came out of the readers digest "@Work" section in their November 2011 issue.

"At work today, I was making a profit-and-loss spreadsheet. "Great, we're in the red!" my boss shouted when he saw it. Then I pointed out that red was bad. "Oh" he said, "I always get those mixed up."

Business people today are trying to over simplify. This is a fatal mistake. Business is complicated. To think Exhibitors can forecast their business by looking at one, two or even a dozen metrics is foolish. No one can predict where the economy is going by only looking at the Dow Jones Industrial Average and Exhibitors can't predict where the company is going by looking at shipments or revenue or even the bottom line.

While working at Whirlpool Corporation I surveyed the top executives of the company asking them what metrics they looked at. The vast majority of the executives looked at less than 5 metrics daily and none of the metrics were macroeconomic in nature. (sidebar - in an interview with Abby Cohen of Goldman Sachs who at that time was considered one of the best traders in the world, she stated that on a daily basis she looked at a minimum of 80 specific metrics.) Back to Whirlpool, being the worlds largest manufacturer of appliances one would think they would have their finger on the pulse of numbers related to; new and existing home sales, housing starts & construction spending (*since this directly effects sales*), oil prices (*since this directly affects logistics costs*), paper prices (*since this directly affects packaging*), commodity prices like copper even steel (*since this directly affects production costs*), interest rates and exchange rates (*since they are a global company dealing in multiple currencies*). Sadly, on a daily basis these execs looked at rear view mirror data like; the number of units shipped and the revenue generated for cash flow from the previous day. So it is no wonder that when the economy took a nose dive they were not prepared and found themselves scrambling to survive like many other companies (in fairness, they have survived for a long time.

If someone is getting paid to strategically direct a company they should learn how to look at the numbers in such a way that they can see trends and understand volatility and protect the company from crisis conditions. I asked one executive why he didn't do more predictive activity and he said "if I go to a Board of Directors meeting and tell them that we are taking actions to downsize, pull back on production and hold cash because the next year is going to be a really rough, they would crucify me. It is easier to explain to them that the economic conditions are the reason we are faltering and to tell them what we are doing to in response to weather the storm. When I do that I am a hero and typically rewarded as such."

Alan Greenspan once said that the price of paper, cardboard and cardboard production were typically good indicators of the end of a bear market because companies typically start to ramp back up by ordering more packaging. Oddly enough throughout this recession I have yet to have an executive I have spoken to mention that he or she has been tracking cardboard prices.

The old expression *figures lie and liars figure,* is a half truth. People are fooled by numbers if they only see part of them. If they read the fine print one can usually see through the scams of the world. But most executives today are too busy micromanaging and asking for one page summaries of complex, multifaceted issues. Unfortunately management that isn't making data driven decisions is doomed. But that is changing because there is a revolution happening and data is leading the way. LSS Exhibitors stop looking for one page summaries and start digging into data. They look at trends and look as far backards and forwards as they can. They do this because LSS is a sound way of looking at and managing a business for continuous improvement.

Winston Churchill said "Democracy is the worst form of government, except for every other form of government." The same holds true of Lean Six Sigma. It is the worst methodology for continuous improvement, except for every other form of continuous improvement. Will it be here tomorrow? I hope not, because if it isn't, whatever takes it place would have to be pretty darn good, even amazing.

So by this point an Exhibitor should have been through a pretty complete cycle of the DIMAIC having; defined their goals and objective, implemented a show where they measured specific x's and noises using the data for analysis where they found root causes of the issues. Ultimately their analysis should be driving them to take some steps toward improvement by executing some experiments that they plugged back into the define phase to start the cycle over at the next show. This iterative process is the best thing on the market. It is what separates the successful LSS Exhibitor from the rest of the herd because it delivers cost reductions, revenue increases and higher ROI.

The DIMAIC is iterative but it also has some closure. In the world outside of exhibiting the Control phase is designed as a stage to bring closure to projects and also to support continuous monitoring and improvement. But the exhibiting world is different. Inside the exhibiting world most Exhibitors have a cycle of shows they do and the cycle repeats on a schedule. Unlike the manufacturing world or the financial transactional world or almost any other world, the Exhibitor world changes cycle to cycle. Most Exhibitors feel strongly that their Target Attendees want a different look and feel from their booth space from one year to the next. These Exhibitors get fearful that the Attendees will see the same old booth and move on down the aisle. So they counter this by changing everything. The bigger the Exhibitor the more changes they make. LSS Exhibitor use this cycle of change as an opportunity to experiment which means they change some things that can be experimented on without negatively affecting the Purchase Experience. They also change things in relationship to their goals and objectives.

As one product or service offering is moving from the Awareness stage to the Consideration stage they introduce another offering and create awareness around it. Simultaneously they will have offerings in conversion activities and will keep the booth fresh with new bundling options or show specials. The booth becomes their laboratory and they use it well. They don't waste a single opportunity to advance their learnings.

Control phase objectives;
- Prepare a plan that documents and controls improvements made
- Implement a transition plan
- Transition product or service offerings from one stage to another
- Document key learnings, results, savings, revenue improvements
- Thank Champions, sponsors
- Reward team members
- Close-out the project
- Celebrate successes with the team
- Monitor the key factors

One of the main reasons that LSS Exhibitors are so successful is that they clearly see the process of the exhibit world and they control the process. They work their offerings through the stages of the Purchase Experience;

- Awareness
- Consideration
- Preference
- Conversion

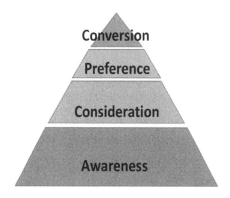

An they use the tools of the DIMAIC to understand that the **DESIGN DRIVES BEHAVIOR.** Meaning they understand the impact of the extrinsic value adders, external value adders and high touch points. They also understand the cognitive process of decision making. They verify the effect of every piece of booth property, every costume/article of clothing and every staff greeting. They know how to observe and make changes so that the Purchase Experience is satisfying for the Attendee every time.

Value Streams				
Pyramid Sales Phase	Extrinsic Value Streams	Intrinsic Value Streams	Relational (High)	Exhibitor Booth
PE Phase	Form	Function	TouchPoints	Activity
Awareness	Sight/Taste	Information	Samples	Presentation
Consideration	Sound	Application	Engagement	Demonstration
Preference	Touch	Education	Interaction	Objections
Conversion	Scent/Taste	Consultation	Affirmation	Invitation

Satisfying because, one of the things LSS Exhibitors learn is how to use the methods of cultural anthropologists to become great observers of the subculture associated with each show they exhibit at. They see below the surface and understand the norms, habits, lifestyles and nuances of the Attendees at these events and they are immersed in their culture. They speak their language, recognize their local heros, abide by their rituals and customs and find ways to match their Target Attendees in order to strengthen the bonds that drive loyal, lifetime advocacy. In short they clearly hear the harmonious voice of their Customer. They are in tune with it as it resonates through their organizations and projects itself in their exhibit spaces. Consequently they experiment with the factors that respond to the Customer voices.

They spend the time to become experts in development of the Purchase Experiences by experimenting with it instead of using observational information recklessly. They "tour" the show floors of the shows they exhibit at as well as the show floors of seemingly unrelated events and they actively observe these experiences. They become so immersed in their work that every place they go they observe and document the Purchase Experience around them and they use the things they note as factors for experiments in their laboratories.

They look at and map out locations, they examine the private languages and unspoken languages (body language) of the participants. They observe the rituals, ceremonies and rites of passage of the people involved. They learn how they think and the process they go through when connecting and when making decisions. They see what behaviors are accepted and what behaviors are shunned or taboo. In essence they become Cultural Anthropologists and Ethnographers. Instead of just copying what other exhibitors do, they use the items and ideas they observe as factors in their experimental laboratory. They use their science attributes to verify their artistic characteristics.

The Control Step

During the Improve phase, solutions and ideas are generated, evaluated and even implemented. This often involves a reloop by conducting experiments (DOE's) to trace and confirm the stability of the implemented improvements. Consequently formal process controls tools are utilized to provide standardization and verification. For example LSS Exhibitors often implement a training program for the staff with an SOP (standard operating procedure) to ensure that no elements of the training are overlooked. In some settings statistical tools like control charts (SPC) can indicate whether a process operating within an acceptable range and if it is being influenced by "common cause" variation, factors and noises. Continuous improvement requires attitional tools such as control plans and capability studies.

Control Plan

The Control Plan is a tool used to ensure that the improvements continue. The Control Plan is a simple document that clarifies the process details regarding the inputs and outputs which the Improve phase has developed. By monitoring the process one can see if it strays out of control and use the tools to adjust it. If there are long-term action items the project list and possibly a Gantt Chart can be updated and followed until corrective actions are complete. Here is a sample of a Control Plan that is utilized to document the information.

Control Plan														
Process Step	CTQ	Specification Description		LSL	USL	Measurement Units	Measurement	Sample Size	Frequency of Measurement	Who Responsible	Where Data Resides	SOP	Data Type	Measurement Method

Capability Studies

The capability study is one of the tools of Lean Six Sigma that helps Exhibitors understand what their process can do and the probability of the process producing errors or defects. It does this through the use of two specific metrics; Cp-process capability number, Cpk-process capability index. The two metrics measure the capability of the system in meeting specification.

As stated earlier the two main objectives of Lean Six Sigma are to center the process to the target, and/or reduce the spread or variability of the system The capability study tells exactly how far Exhibitors are from their Lean Six Sigma targets or objectives. It lets them know if their process is centered and it also tells how much variability the process has compared to some specified limits or band of tolerance.

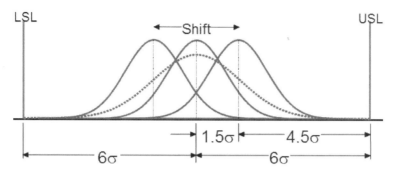

Specifically **Cp** tells how good the process variation is compared to the specification or tolerance. It compares the process spread to the tolerance spread (hopefully as defined by the Customer). It is often said that Cp indicates if all the darts you are throwing are grouped together and Cpk tells if the group of darts are centered on the bullseye.

For example suppose an Exhibitor designs a Purchase Experience process that entails the use of scheduled upper level management meetings with Target Attendees. They have 15 executive and the meetings take 15 minutes each, therefore each executive could have 4 meetings per hour. Potentially they can have about (15*4=60), 60 meetings an hour. Prior to the show they decided that they couldn't possibly have that many meetings because it was difficult to get Target Attendees and managers to commit to meeting during the show so they decided to shoot for a little over half of that or 32 meetings per hour plus or minus 1.

So off they go to the show where they collected their data. As it turned out the show data revealed that they averaged 32 meetings an hour which was right on target but there was a real spread in the efficiency of the meeting process and they saw that the standard deviation of the meetings was .394. So how efficient were they and how did they do in terms of capability.

To summarize;

- Mean = 32 Target Attendee meetings per hour (Sometimes the Exhibitor had 60 meetings but other times they only had one or two in an hour.)
- Std. Deviation = (0.394 Target Attendees) There was a dispersion of the number of meetings because some Attendees didn't show up. Sometime the managers went over, sometimes managers took a break or didn't come back from a break fast enough, later in the day it was harder to fill the schedule...etc.
- Specification = 32 +/- 1 The goal for Target Attendee meetings per hour was to get more than half of the meeting time filled.
- Upper Specification limit = 32 + 1=33
- Lower Specification limit = 32 -1=31

At a first glance at the data it's easy to jump to the conclusion that they are hitting the target about half the time since on average they are getting 32 meetings per hour. But the mean is misleading here and the Cp tells a different story so let's calculate it.

The formula for calculating Cp = (USL-LSL)/(6*St.Dev.) where USL = upper spec limit, LSL = lower spec limit, St. Dev = standard deviation. In the example they would get (33 - 31) / 6 x 0.394. This gives a Cp = 0.846 about 84% efficiency, which sounds pretty good, yes there is room for improvement but it is certainly a better indicator than the mean was. If they wanted to convert the Cp to a sigma level we multiple it by 3. This means that a Cp of 1 would give a 3 sigma process and a Cp of 2 would give a 6 sigma process. For the example above, the process variation can be considered to have a sigma level of about 2.5 which means for every million opportunities they fail 158655 times per the table.

Process Sigma Table

Defects per Million Opportunities	Sigma Level	Process Yield Py
933193	0.00	6.700000
841300	0.500	15.900000
691462	**1.000**	**30.900000**
500000	1.500	50.000000
308538	2.000	69.100000
158655	*2.500*	*84.100000*
66807	3.000	93.300000
10724	3.80	98.900000
6210	4.00	99.400000
1350	4.50	99.870000
233	5.00	99.980000
32	5.50	99.996800
2	6.00	99.999660

Cp is a measure of how tight or loose the process is based on the center of the specifications. The higher the value the narrower the spread (more precise) of the process.

So, if they take the example above and say the process mean is 35 meetings while the standard deviation and specification remains the same the Cp would be the same because the spec target is still 32. It only cares that the specification tolerance is +/- 1, making the total tolerance 2 meetings. Cp is a good metric for judging internally how tight the process is, but it does not tell how well the process conforms to the Target Attendee or Customer's specifications. LSS Exhibitors use Cpk to make that correlation.

When doing a capability study using Cpk, it measures how well the process is centered as well as how much variation there is in it. This is what the Target Attendees will be interested in because it shows how well the process conforms to the specs and the probability of making defects.

Cp and Cpk are coined as "within subgroup", measurements because they use a smoothing estimate for sigma and should measure common cause variation within the subgroup. Capability indices, Cp and Cpk, help assess the changes over a period of time. The goal is to have a high Cp indicating tight process controls and also a centered process (high Cpk).

Capability Study steps;
1. Decide on the characteristic being assessed or measured. Such as length, dwell time, queue time, distance.
2. Validate the specification limits and possibly a target value provided by Target Attendees.
3. Collect and record the data per the DCP (Data Collection Plan).
4. Assess process stability using a control charts
5. If the process is stable, assess the "Normality" of the data.
6. Calculate the basic statistics such as the mean, standard deviation, and variance. Calculate the capability indices (Cp, Cpk) as applicable.
7. Verify to the customer requirement for capability where the process is acceptable.

Processes that are in control should have a process capability that is near the process performance. Significant gaps between capability and performance often indicate special causes. It is possible to have data that falls outside the specification limits (LSL,USL) and still have a capable process. This is all a part of gathering the Voice of the Customer (VOC), the dynamics of customer needs and expectations forces the Exhibitor to continually check the limits and acceptability levels longitudinally.

Recommendation and Data Reports

One of the most important parts of any control element of a project is the reporting out of data. It can be very difficult to satisfy all of the different needs and levels of needs required for reporting especially in a large organization.

Once the analysis is done and the improvement ideas have been gathered they need to be communicated. This is critical to getting the improvements and experiments back into the DIMAIC cycle for evaluation. Using the experimentation plan, FRD and Poka Yoke can help to get everyone on board and moving in the same direction. It can also help to build momentum and as a "thank you" to the organization for the support and persistence in staying on task.

In the measure phase charts and graphs revealed the importance of visceral cognition. Visual elements help management to make connections and progress the learnings. Also simple tables (like the one on the next page) help to get the message across in a clear concise manner.

Results Evaluator		
Evaluating Results	Did we get acceptable Results - YES	Did we get acceptable Results - NO
Did we follow our plan? YES		
Did we follow our plan? NO		

Report formats can vary greatly from organization to organization but a good problem capture document is the A3. This tool follows the Edward Demming - Plan, Do, Check, Act loop (PDCA).

	Process Step/Description:		Date:	Name:	
Plan	Step 1 Theme/Background What is the problem? What pain is it causing? What do you need people to understand? How serious is it? What is the impact? What are you trying to do?			Step 5 Improve What are you going to do to fix it? What are the countermeasures? How are you going to move from As-Is to To-Be Condition? What 5-10 steps can you take to eliminate the root causes?	Do
	Step 2 As-Is Condition What is the current state or condition? What does the process map or value stream map show? Where is it in the flow? How do you verify the problem? What data is there to verify the issue? Is the data reliable?			Step 6 Implement When are you going to do it? What resources are needed? Who will be responsible for what items/tasks? What do you want them to do? How will you execute the changes?	
	Step 3 Root Cause Analysis What data and subsequent analysis has been done? Have you used tools such as; fishbone diagrams, 5 Why, pareto charts, Cause-Effect diagram, FMEA?			Step 7 Evaluate During execution are you meeting the performance results? Do you seem to be moving the needle in the right direction? Did you get the symptoms and root causes right? Did you get the right information?	Check
	Step 4 To-Be Condition What is the target state or condition you would like to aim for? What is acceptable to the organization? What is the acceptable level? Is it on the migration plan with paths in place? What are your measurement expectations for success? How does this impact the CTQ's/CSF's?			Step 8 Control and Follow-up 30, 60, 90 days later ask: Were all action items completed? Is it achieving the expected results? Did it work or didn't it? Is this a long-term fix? Were mistakes made and do you need to reloop?	Act

The A3 is a useful root cause analysis tool but it is also great for communicating the control phase aspects of a project because it captures;

- the problem statement
- the current state condition
- the root cause analysis performed

- the conclusions made
- the improvements implemented
- the follow-up steps needed and control elements required

It serves as a great living record of the project and learnings from the laboratory activities of events, in order to guide the learnings for future projects and create closure to the Lean Six Sigma process for continous improvement.

Now that you have completed the full cycle of the LSS process it should be clear that there is a great deal more to learn and a great deal of work to be done. These tools and methodology are only good if you take them and put them into action. You must use them to become proficient at being good at driving continous improvement.

At the end of the day the DIMAIC process for Exhibitors can be used as a backbone for project management and advancing learnings in order to provide a fantastic Purchase Experience for Target Attendees.

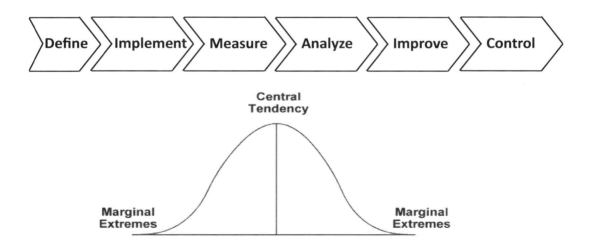

Ch. 8

How to Get an Orange Belt

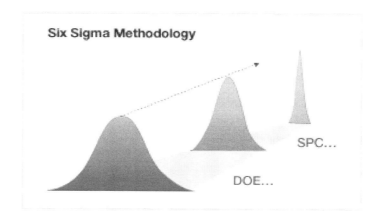

How does someone get an Orange Belt?

Step 1. The first and probably most difficult part has just been accomplished by reading this book. By read this book an Exhibitor is now armed with the understanding of the process and tools required to be an LSS Orange Belt Exhibitor and the next step is easy by comparison.

Step 2. The certification process starts when the Exhibitor starts doing an LSS structured project and using the DIMAIC tools to document and work through a show. By using these tools as a part of the Exhibitor's job they will improve their skill sets and their Purchase Experience. If Exhibitors feel that they are missing something and/or that they are unsure of how to use certain tools look at the sample projects on the website (www.bbmgo.com) and find examples from other LSS Exhibitors of tools they have used and projects they have completed.

Step 3. As part of the DIMAIC process have regular project reviews with the Exhibitor team or and go through the tools and updates for the show.

Review :
- Thought Maps
- Process Maps
- Control Charts (NEM,MSE)
- Statistical Tolerancing
- Designed Experiments
- OFAT
- Full Factorials
- Fractional Factorials
- Resources

- Philosophy
- Level Setting
- Analysis
- ANOVA
- Components of Variance
- Factor Relationship Diagram
- Noise Strategies
- Blocking
- Randomization
- Repeats
- Resolution

Step 4. The Exhibitor next submits the required documentation as evidence that they are performing the work in line with LSS standards.

Step 6. The Exhibitor will be contacted for an interview by a Master Black Belt who will help with any issues and/or answer any questions. If there are no major issues the Master Black Belt will submit the Exhibitor as a candidate for certification.

Step 7. The LSS panel will review the submitted work and the comments from the Master Black Belt and either award a certification or request additional information.

Step 8. If awarded a certification, the Exhibitor will be presented with a certificate from their Master Black Belt or Sensei.

Step 9. Once an Exhibitor is certified their name and credentials will be place on the bbmgo website as recognition and also to provide forward thinking LSS Exhibitors with a mechanism to network with each other. There are also job posting there for companies looking for LSS candidates. From that point on Exhibitors are free to pursue additional belts (Black Belt, Master Black Belt, Sensei) and they are also free to participate in webinars, blogs and all other open forum sessions with other LSS Exhibitors through the **B**uyingBe**h**aviorMETR**ICS** portals such as; www.bbmgo.com.

It's that easy!

Define | Implement | Measure | Analyze | Improve | Control

Martin P. Smith founded BuyingBehavior**METRICS** as a Lean Six Sigma based research and analysis firm committed to providing measurement driven customer solutions to business applications. His main areas of focus are marketing factors such as the shopping environment, cognitive decision making, product and service offering presentation, sensory stimuli and pricing that influence the Purchase Experience down to the consumer level. He is considered to be the leading subject matter expert regarding *"Purchase Experience Behavior"*. (Check out his book THE NEW EXHIBITOR)

Mr. Smith attained the level of Lean Six Sigma Master Black Belt Sensei and as such is an expert in analysis and experimentation in complex, chaotic environments.

He has helped corporations develop disciplined marketing, sales, pricing and promotions processes in an effort to increase value, drive revenue higher and therefore maximize ROI. These endeavors have resulted in hundreds of millions of dollars in revenue generation and savings which have been meticulously documented.

He has extensive experience increasing quality due to his view of transactional venues as products produced in the "corporate factory" that affect the reference value of Consumers and Attendees as they move through their purchasing decisions.

He has a BS in Mechanical Engineering from Illinois Institute of Technology. He is the recipient of the 2006 ISBM Academic Practitioners award at the Kellogg Business School for work related to Bayesian and Markov Modeling in event venues.

He can be contacted at 269-313-0998 or *msmith@bbmgo.com.*